Thought Dreams

Other Books by Michael Albert

What Is To Be Undone

Unorthodox Marxism (with Robin Hahnel)

Marxism and Socialist Theory (with Robin Hahnel)

Socialism Today and Tomorrow (with Robin Hahnel)

Liberating Theory (with Leslie Cagan, Noam Chomsky, Robin   Hahnel, Mel King, Lydia Sargent, Holly Sklar)

The Quiet Revolution in Welfare Economics (with Robin Hahnel)

The Political Economy of Participatory Economics (with Robin Hahnel)

Looking Forward (with Robin Hahnel)

Stop the Killing Train

Thinking Forward

Moving Forward

Trajectory of Change

Parecon: Life After Capitalism

Thought Dreams
Radical Theory for the Twenty-First Century

Michael Albert

ARBEITER RING PUBLISHING • WINNIPEG

Arbeiter Ring Publishing
201E-121 Osborne St.
Winnipeg, Manitoba
Canada R3L 1Y4
info@arbeiterring.com
www.arbeiterring.com/

Printed in Canada by the workers at Hignell Printing.

Cover design by Mike Carroll
Cover image by tamara rae Biebrich

Financial assistance of the Manitoba Arts Council/Conseil des Arts du Manitoba.

Canada Council   Conseil des Arts
for the Arts   du Canada

MANITOBA arts COUNCIL
CONSEIL DES   DU MANITOBA

National Library of Canada Cataloguing in Publication

Albert, Michael, 1947-

Thought dreams : radical theory for the 21st century / Michael Albert.

ISBN 1-894037-10-3

1. Sociology   I. Title.

HM585.A42 2004   301   C2004-900093-4

If my thought dreams could be seen, they'd probably put my head in a guillotine.

– Bob Dylan

Contents

Preface

I teach a course with the name Radical Theory each summer at the Z
Media Institute (ZMI) which is sponsored by *Z Magazine*. ZMI exists to teach social theory, analysis, vision, strategy, and particularly
media skills to students from around the world. It lasts ten days, is
very intense, and has been a remarkable experience for roughly 650
graduates to date. You can find out more about ZMI at *Z*'s web site,
ZNet, at http://www.zmag.org.

The ZMI Radical Theory course has three sessions, each an hour
and a half. I also taught a course with the same name on the World
Wide Web. The online course, no longer given, was an outgrowth of
the ZMI course. This book is, in turn, an outgrowth of the online
course. The process went like this: after teaching ZMI a few times, I
had the course videotaped and later transcribed. The material was
enlarged and adapted into ten lectures for the online course, which
also involved considerable discussion in online forums. The ten online
lectures plus some of the discussion have been massaged into this
book. The chapters here are chatty, without footnotes, and make no
pretense at precision. They are informal lectures and we have tried to
capture an element of student participation by including material in
quotes, but without attribution.

The ZMI and online courses and this book all try to display the spirit and process of thinking about radical theory, vision, and strategy. We develop a particular theory, do some specific visionary thinking, and propose some modest strategic ideas. While the process is the first-order priority, the content is important too, and a second priority. Still, usually one presents a set of views in a linear fashion—moving from point to point, finishing one thing before beginning the next. In this book, we instead circle back and forth around aspects of the whole picture. We don't present it as a finished conception but instead construct a perspective as one might in actual practice. It's messier, and much of that messiness is critical to understanding the process and has been retained.

This is the second lecture-compendium book I have published with Arbeiter Ring, the first being *Thinking Forward* which deals with constructing economic vision. I should like to thank the people at Arbeiter, and particularly ria julien, for feeling that this material is valuable and effective, and for their editorial aid. We are true to the original, retaining as much of its spontaneity as we could preserve.

I must also point out that while this book's specific words are entirely my responsibility, the insights have many and varied sources. Some are mine. Many are jointly mine and Robin Hahnel's, my frequent co-author. Still others, more numerous, are products of the Left more broadly. For those I am a scribe only.

I do hope you find this book empowering and are able to take its lessons further in your own thought and deeds.

1. What's a Theory

The Argentine writer Jorge Luis Borges tells a tale of a man cursed not only with the ability to remember every leaf, every wave, every pattern of shadows that he has ever seen but also with the inability to realize that different leaves are united by the concept 'leaf' or that the myriad shifting shapes of the waves are all examples of the one idea of 'wave.' This extreme fragmentation of experience is the antithesis of man's inherent need to find unifying themes in nature. The great scientists have often been those who saw such themes where others failed, who saw wave, under the waves.

–Brian Silver

Theories are collections of concepts about some real world area of interest that facilitate explaining, predicting, or intervening. Theories explain why and how things occur as they do. We use them to predict what may happen given the way things are. We choose ways of acting to influence outcomes as we desire.

Some theories are better for one purpose, worse for others. Darwin's theory of natural selection, for example, explains very well, predicts barely at all, and allows intervention of only a quite limited sort. Theories of the solar system, based on Newtonian gravity, not only explain but also very precisely predict, for example, where a planet will be on some day, and even some hour, fifty years from now. Social theories generally explain, predict, and permit intervention, none with perfect confidence, but each with enough reliability to be more useful than just winging it, instead.

So what do we want in the way of theory?

As radicals, we want a theory that explains social events and trends sufficiently for us to situate ourselves, explain to others, and understand the way things are. We want a theory to predict phenomena, and give us a notion of what's coming. Finally, we want a theory to help seek outcomes we desire. How do we develop such a theory?

Theories are built with concepts. So what is a concept?

It's an assumption.

Well, yes, sometimes.

It's a word, a label.

Yes, for our purposes a concept is just a name for something. A concept is—well we can perhaps best define it by giving examples. Is atom a concept? Is electron a concept? Is income a concept? Is full employment a concept? Yes, but what makes them concepts?

They are names, labels?

Yes, they are names of things we think are out in the real world and which we have isolated from the whole of reality and given a separate name or identity. Of the masses of interconnected stuff in the world, we want to pay special attention to some parts. We want our theory to highlight those parts. And so we have concepts to name parts or features or aspects that we especially want to keep track of.

Consider an example of a concept inside the human body. What is one?

How about blood pressure?

Yes, or the circulatory system. That's a concept. But what could we call a person's head plus her left wrist? We don't have a name for that. The head plus left wrist exists in the world and we could give it a name if we chose to, but we haven't done that, as far as I know. You could have a name for the head plus the left wrist as a way to organize data when thinking about the biology of human beings. But it turns out it is silly to combine the head and left wrist and name it "hrist," because we don't have any interest in tracking the dynamics of the hrist. The hrist doesn't come into play as an entity useful to focus on when trying to explain, predict, or intervene in human biology.

What is the difference, then, between head plus left wrist, or hrist, and the bunches of tubes strung through the body, some in my wrist and others in my head, that we name the circulatory system? Why is one ridiculous to pick out as a concept, and the other very appropriate?

The difference is that the circulatory system has characteristics and attributes relevant to understanding human beings to intervene in health. That's what conceptual work is about: looking at reality and putting a label on some features useful to track. Tree is a concept, but largest branch plus oldest leaf isn't a concept. Perhaps it sounds stupid put so crassly, largest branch plus oldest leaf, but this is quite important. The idea in this process is that we try to highlight things that facilitate analysis and prediction and help in guiding practice.

Now consider the economic concept "exchange value." It's roughly what most people call price. The exchange value of a product is what that product trades for. And in different theories, the actual amount an item trades for, relative to what another item trades for, will be explained in different ways. But what value an item trades for is itself a concept.

How about the color of the item?

Exchange value is a concept that we use in economic theory. Color is not a concept that we use in economic theory. Economists don't care about how many of each item are which color, so they don't highlight color in their theory. You can pick up any economics book and look forever and you won't find color in the theoretical apparatus. Color of items is not a useful focus to bring into prime viewing territory in our economic intellectual tool box. It isn't that color doesn't exist. Products are colored. It isn't that we can't make color a concept. We could make it a concept. It is that we choose not to make it an economic concept, though we do use it in design and other domains. And economists could be wrong, of course, and if they are wrong their theory will be poorer as a result of leaving out color as a featured concept. But if they are right, as I think they are, then not wasting time tracking color is a sensible choice.

So we see that to create theory we develop concepts from the whole interwoven tapestry of the real world and we use them to answer questions about why and how things happen, about what we can expect to happen, and about how we might affect what happens. When looking at interrelations among our chosen concepts doesn't fully answer our questions, we define more concepts or adapt those we are using. Our theory, then, is our understanding of how our various concepts affect one another and move dynamically over time.

Okay, what's the name of some social theories radicals use to understand the world in order to intervene to make it better?

Marxism?

Feminism?

Yes, Marxism and feminism, also nationalism is another one, and anarchism is a fourth framework radicals critical of existing relations use to understand, predict, and try to guide actions.

Call these things theories, call them intellectual frameworks, call them whatever you want, but the point is that they are tools for looking at reality, organizing our thoughts, and prioritizing what we highlight, based on concepts. You can think of each framework as a helpmate that we carry around with us. We use the helpmate's apparatus and concepts to try to explain, predict, and guide practice.

Okay, since theories are built on concepts, what are the concepts of these different intellectual frameworks or theories? For example, what are some of the key concepts associated with Marxism?

Class struggle?

Economics?

Certainly class struggle is one, and so is class itself. Economy is another, and so is alienation, exploitation, commodity, relations of production, ownership relations, exchange value, use value, profit rate, and so on. We don't need to closely detail what all these mean, and perhaps you have only heard some of them, but just keep these key Marxist concepts and your impression of what they broadly refer to in the back of your mind.

Continuing, what are some anarchist concepts?

Hierarchy?

Mutual aid?

Well, hierarchy certainly is one. Perhaps mutual aid, but certainly authoritarianism and also perhaps decentralization. Certainly the state, dictatorship, and laws.

Let's continue. What are concepts of feminism?

Patriarchy?

Patriarchy is a key feminist concept, sure. What else?

Gender, sexuality, sexism.

Of course. But we had class up there in Marxism. What could we have added for Marxism that's a derivative of class? What's the top class in our society?

Capitalist?

Clearly it works top down: capitalist, worker, and maybe some other classes, too. And in anarchism we could contrast the authority figure, the person at the top of the hierarchy, the order-giver (maybe the dictator or president) with the order-taker. What about in feminism? What are some concepts like these found in feminism?

Man and woman?

Man and woman, exactly, or other gendered or sex-defined roles. For example, mother and father are roles that emerge from social structures more or less in the same way worker, manager, and owner do. Any society will have adults relating to children, just as any society will have people engaging in economic activity. But the particular ways these things occur, with women and men mothering and fathering in sex-defined ways, or with people at work carrying out orders, giving orders, or running the whole show, are socially determined. There are women and men in the world, and what defines a woman versus what defines a man, as well as the different major roles they occupy are critically important for feminists. Some non-feminist theories, in contrast, say there are just people and don't highlight that there are two genders or other kinship and sex-related differences. This can be okay, for some purposes. Other times it's not okay, however, and in history actually many theorists failed to incorporate sex, gender, and kinship differences out of a sexist denial that there is anyone other than men, and their theories suffered due to this conceptual weakness, of course.

Finally, what about nationalism? What are some of the key concepts in nationalism?

Nation, ethnicity, race?

Yes, and also religion and specific instances of these, for sure. Maybe communities; culture; modes of celebration, communication, and identification are additional concepts and types of relations among these.

Like racism?

Yes, and ethnocentrism, apartheid, and so on.

Now the very interesting thing in this enumeration of concepts, even at this very introductory level, even without going in to the details of what each concept means, is that these various theories are all about understanding the same world and about trying to change that same world for the better, and yet their intellectual tool boxes are very different. If we had four different chalkboards and we asked members of each orientation to list the eight or ten primary concepts in their orientation, there would be little overlap, perhaps none at all. And if we detailed what the concepts mean, even when there is apparent overlap between concepts, it would turn out they have different meanings in each framework. So what's happening?

Different motivations?

Yes, all these folks are looking at the same world. They're doing theory. They're trying to look at that world and develop concepts that focus on what's important to facilitate their thinking in accord with their priorities. So, we have to ask ourselves, why are the concepts so different? Is the reason concepts differ among these orientations because some approaches are stupid and others smart? Are some of the approaches just making it up, so their concepts don't correspond to reality? Or do the different approaches have different priorities causing them to generate different concepts? Are they legitimately trying to accomplish different things, so they sensibly highlight and leave out different features?

Let's go back and ask about each framework, what might cause it to look like it does. How come Marxism has the central concepts it has, but it doesn't have mothering, fathering, woman, man, sexism, race, ethnicity, religion and many other possible basic concepts at its core? It doesn't mean that these phenomena never show up for a Marxist, but they are not the basic concepts employed when the Marxist looks at society and history. Why?

Because they aren't about class struggle?

Sure, but so what? Why does class struggle matter most to the Marxist?

Because Marx wrote it that way?

Well, yes, the thing we call Marxism has the concepts it has because Marx and others put them in. But, other than that Marx wrote it that way, what else might explain Marxism's choice of concepts?

Well, Marxism focuses in on class and the economy. Why might it do that? It could be because Marxists look at the world and to them it seems that economy is the most important thing. Economy runs the show. They feel that if they focus their concepts on the economy, secondary concepts about other phenomena can come later. Having their central concepts focus on economic relations will give them a theory that gets to the heart of matters quickest.

There is another possible reason, however. Suppose my personal interests are somehow more correlated to economy than to anything else. My choice of core concepts could be due to an honest objective assessment (whether right or wrong) that economics is most important for explanation, prediction, and intervention regarding everything that is social or historical. But the choice could also be due to a more subjective assessment stemming from the limitations and pressures that I myself feel in my own life, which might not be entirely representative of society more broadly. It could be that I didn't even take into account the possibility that other factors are historically comparably important to economics, merely because they aren't comparably important to me in my personal life, or because I don't want to look at them closely because if I did, it would be damaging to my interests. Think about male thinkers ignoring gender, for example.

Let's use another example outside of the radical realm to try to clarify this key point. What's neoclassical economics?

It's a name that's given to the economic theory that's taught in universities. And that theory, too, has various concepts such as supply and demand, marginal utility, preference ordering, and you have probably heard of some of the concepts—employment, inflation, market, and so on.

Now, if the goal of that theory is to understand the effect of economics on human beings, we can guess there will be a concept human. You can't have a theory that's supposed to understand something, if that thing isn't one of the concepts of the theory. Theories are about their concepts. If there is no concept human, then there is no attention given specifically to humans, just as if there is no concept hrist, there is no attention given to the specific combination head plus left wrist.

So, okay, we intuit that there will be a neoclassical economics concept "human" and we'll see in it, presumably, all the various attributes of humans that could be affected by the economy. But it turns out if you actually look at bourgeois economics, surprisingly you don't find that. Humans in the rich and complex sense that would include everything about them that can be affected by economics, aren't in the theory as a basic concept. Neoclassical economics doesn't include the many ways that humans are changed by the workplace and highlight how it occurs and its reflexive implications back on the economy. Nor does neoclassical economics recognize that humans are changed by market transactions or explain how. Nor does it highlight how humans are changed by income distribution, patterns of ownership, levels of employment, or divisions of labor. It doesn't have a concept of humans that includes all the various facets that economic phenomena impact. It doesn't highlight and track affected facets, such as our consciousness, our feelings, our integrity, our skills and talents, our sense of solidarity, our empowerment, and even our physical well-being, which are certainly economically relevant, both affected and having effects, we would likely agree.

Instead neoclassical economic theory says just that inputs are transformed into outputs, inputs being the material things we combine in our labors and the work itself, and outputs being the cars or other products. Humans in all their many variants and conditions aren't present, only their labor is. The theory, in other words, has a certain purpose and leaves out things not bearing on that purpose. In this case it leaves out much of what constitutes being human and how being human is impacted by economic activity and outcomes that affect our personalities, our dignity, our levels of fulfillment and self esteem, our consciousness, confidence, and skills, and so on. And it also leaves out the inverse impact of our varied human features on economic relations. This leaving-out is called abstracting.

Every theory abstracts away some things and puts other things into priority following largely from the way it settles on preferred concepts. And there is nothing wrong per se, we should realize, with including and excluding features, or abstracting. Every theory must do it. But while a theory can leave out something sensibly, because it isn't consequential (such as hrist), a theory can also leave out something wrongly—something which actually is consequential. And it might do this by oversight, making an honest mistake. There was a time when physics didn't even have the concept electron, due to honest ignorance. But a theory could also leave out something important because it literally wants to leave it out, either because the thing is peripheral to or is contrary to the theorist's interests, though not to honestly understanding the reality in question. Thus the practitioners of the theory may want to leave something out because it is something they themselves don't want to pay attention to, for example, the plight of workers in the workplace. Or they may leave something out in order to obscure anyone else paying attention to it, for example, the potential power of workers functioning as a class.

So the question arises, why might the practitioners of neoclassical economics want to leave out the effect of economics on people's personalities? Well, of course, once we ask the question we have already answered it.

Because highlighting that would make it hard to rationalize the harmful effects of the economy away.

Exactly. Neoclassical economists claim they are trying to understand the economy, but that's really an exaggeration. They are trying to talk about the economy in a way that will seem appropriate and compelling (which means it has to provide some understanding, for sure), but that will in the first place rationalize and justify the current economy as the only possible good economy. And they don't want to highlight anything that might disrupt that outcome.

But what if you're a capitalist and you're keeping track of what is going on in the economy?

You need the truth.

Right. You don't want to rationalize while you're doing business in the boardroom. There you want to get useful, truthful answers to questions that you care about. So you have bookkeeping and management. And these pay attention to things in a different fashion than neoclassical economics. The capitalist goes to business school, not to economics graduate school, and with good reason. The capitalist wants to understand what is going on in the economy and to intervene in order to make a profit, which entails, as we will see later, playing pretty close attention to conditions of the workforce. The neoclassical economist, on the other hand, discusses the same economy, but with a different purpose: to rationalize capitalism as most desirable among all possible options, and then, within that first-order limitation, to understand its operations.

Okay, why is the framework the capitalist uses to think about how to act and what to do organized around profits as the bottom line?

That's their agenda.

Yes, because the pursuit of profits is the capitalist's agenda. So to think in terms of implications for profits is the capitalist's way of looking at the world. He wants to see the world in terms of concepts that let him (or rarely her) accomplish the ends he has in mind.

So why does the capitalist's tool box contain a lot of concepts missing from the neoclassical economist's tool box, and vice versa?

Because understanding the economy so as to be able to make the most profits is not the same as explaining the economy in a way that rationalizes and legitimates it.

Alright, I want to take one more little detour, please. The above is a broad argument, a kind of intimation of a case against neoclassical economics. It is not a complete and full argument. That would take us too far afield. It would require that we closely investigate the economic theory and its concepts and claims and show how they are truncated by the overriding interest of rationalization, as opposed to honestly trying to understand the economy. That is for another time. But I do want to make it a little more credible that what I have claimed about neoclassical economics is in fact the case, so I'll take another example of the same dynamic, but one for which we have a very clear piece of simple and virtually irrefutable evidence.

Consider political theory, the stuff taught in undergraduate and graduate political science departments. It is supposed to be a theory, or conceptual framework, for understanding the workings of political institutions, government, the judiciary, and so on. How are policies made? What pressures come into play? What roles and values guide the outcomes? What can we predict?

Suppose we consider a political science department in the former Soviet Union, circa 1989. And suppose some top general in the Russian politburo, the central governmental policy-making institution, stole volumes of documents that had been secreted away in Russian vaults and made these available publicly. And suppose they were details of policy making during the Stalin purges or the Afghan War, for example.

Now, what would we expect Soviet university political science departments to do?

Look the other way?

Yes, that's quite right. They would ignore the documents. And what would that tell us about those departments?

That they weren't in fact interested in understanding the Soviet government?

Yes, it would tell anyone who wasn't being totally obtuse about it, that those departments didn't exist to understand the actual operations of the Soviet government. Rather, they existed to talk about those operations in ways that had sufficient relation to actual fact to appear credible, but that rationalized the government's choices as moral, wise, etc. The scholars in those Soviet political science departments would have no need to look at the best possible source material, because their purpose was not, in fact, to understand what had actually occurred, or even to document it, but was only to rationalize or obscure it.

I think there isn't a person in the U.S. who couldn't understand this argument, and who wouldn't laugh at a Soviet political scientist trying to explain away the fact that they ignored such materials, assuming they had been readily available.

Okay, let's skip back to the U.S.

During the Vietnam War a fellow named Daniel Ellsberg with super high government security clearance decided that the war was horribly immoral and decided to do something about it. So he entered the secret halls of the U.S. government and he stole documents. He photocopied them in the dead of night, and he made off with the copies. After accumulating volumes of the stuff, he made it public. And in the context of the social pressures of the time, the material was published and became freely available as the *Pentagon Papers*.

And now we come to the punch line.

To my knowledge there is not a political science department in the country where these secret, first hand, direct documents about U.S. policy making at a crucial time in U.S. history are used as primary research material. In fact, there are few if any graduate political science programs where these documents are used at all, much less prominently. In fact, with the exception of analysis by a very few dissident political scientists, the *Pentagon Papers* are essentially removed from the spectrum of materials that are seriously addressed and discussed.

And what does this tell us about the discipline called political science? It tells us just as in the Soviet case, of course, that the departments have as their purpose not firstly to understand political science and particularly the polity of our society, but to rationalize it. In other words, it tells us that just what we claimed for neoclassical economics vis-à-vis the economy holds for political science, except that in the case of political science we have a nearly perfect experiment to bear out the claim without having to first dissect the concepts employed in the field.

So the point of this is to show that an elaborate intellectual framework that is employed by lots of people can be other than what it claims to be. It might claim to offer concepts for understanding some domain from some point of view, say the polity or economy, but it might instead actually contain concepts for understanding it from a different, unstated, point of view, or even just for rationalizing it.

Lest we take wrong conclusions from the above discussion, we may need to briefly reiterate a point before we get back to the radical side of conceptualizing.

Again, there's nothing intrinsically wrong with abstracting. There is nothing wrong with having aims and organizing one's tool box of concepts in light of those aims. Everybody does that. In fact, everybody has to do that because there is no such thing as a comprehensive theory that is perfectly suitable to all ends and perfectly addresses all facets of existence. No one has a theory of anything at all that is that complete. No one has a theory that focuses its users as efficiently for all ends as some other more directed theories focus their users to very specific ends.

Every theory has some focus and some questions it is well suited to address, and others that it ignores. Theories abstract some phenomena and incorporate other phenomena, depending on priorities. Every theory addresses some domain and the types of questions that any theory will most effectively answer will depend on what that theory's users want to be able to understand and affect with it. The problem with capitalists or neoclassical economists or political scientists isn't that they each use a conceptual tool box suited to their needs. We all do that. There is no alternative to doing that. It is that the capitalists' needs—to maximize their profits and power regardless of the impact on others—are vile and immoral. And the neoclassical economists' (or political scientists') needs—to first rationalize the system, and only then, not violating that precept, to understand it—are duplicitous and manipulative. And the problem is that each of these actors claims to be doing something quite different from what they are doing.

Okay, let's go back to the theories we were considering that radicals might use to deal with society and history.

Why does feminism come into being and look the way it does? Why does it have the concepts it has? Somebody who is a strong feminist background answer please—

Because it is interested in a relationship between people?

Yes, but which relationship?

The one between people and men.

People meaning women, I take it, and men meaning what's left? Yes, I suppose I can go with that for the moment. And so whose interests are guiding the choices of this theory?

Women's interests?

Broadly, yes. And so women look at the world from the point of view of their interests and try to name what the important features are and what the key features to keep track of are, and in that way arrive at a set of concepts. Now it shouldn't be surprising that those concepts are going to have a certain tilt, let's call it. And other concepts formed by someone looking at the world but starting out with another set of priorities, are going to have a different tilt. That makes sense.

To avoid controversy but still see the general point, think of a radio. I have a theory of the radio suitable for getting sounds out of it by turning the knob and controlling the volume. My concepts are knob, volume, station, and so on. Someone else has a theory of the radio that gets to the innards of it and permits fixing problems that arise inside. Her concepts might be transistor, diode, or whatever. Another person has a still more basic theory emphasizing electromagnetic waves. We have different purposes so we have different concepts. There is nothing wrong with that as long as we are each true to the reality we are trying to deal with and honest about what we are doing.

Now, apply this recognition to theorizing society. A particular viewpoint may be too narrow in light of some end. Or that same viewpoint might be quite powerful, at least for some priorities.

Our goal in coming chapters is to develop a conceptual tool box for looking at society and history in ways highlighting effects on human beings so as to predict how we can usefully intervene. Next chapter we'll start defining new concepts of our own, building our own new orientation one step at a time.

Meanwhile, consider the following: Does what we have been saying ring true? Does it convey new insights that might clarify certain outstanding questions you have had, or that might raise new useful questions, for that matter?

2. Basic Concepts

That which we know is a little thing; that which we do not know is immense.

–Pierre-Simon de Laplace

The disadvantage of exclusive attention to a group of abstractions, however well-founded, is that, by the nature of the case, you have abstracted from the remainder of things.

–Alfred North Whitehead

We want to build our own worldview or theory. We know we have to stock it with concepts—that is, parts of reality that we are going to pay special attention to in our work. So what are some concepts that we want our theory to have?

Environmentalism?

The ecology?

Yes, you might say environmentalism or the ecology. Sure.

What about sustainability?

Well yes, it is a concept, but it is also a value, and we don't want values now. All we are doing for the moment is finding basic things that are out there in society and history that we want to highlight.

We're not trying to decide what we value or don't value, yet. We just want to know what we need to include in this theory as elements of reality that we wish to focus on.

How about culture?

Do we want to pay attention to culture? Yes, of course we do.

Class?

Yes.

Race?

Certainly.

Sexuality?

I would hope so. And it seems pretty clear that if we go around and keep offering suggestions, we will list pretty much all the things found in those other radical dissident theories that we talked about last lecture. So maybe we can take a shortcut toward our destination by borrowing from those heritages.

What is each of those theory's reason for being, and what can we usefully learn from each? For example, why does Marxism exist as a theory? What is it about the world that breeds Marxism?

Oppression?

Yes, true enough, but what kind of oppression?

Class oppression?

Yes, and so there is something about the world that divides us into groups, one of which has an interest in understanding the economy from the point of view of Marxism. Which group is that?

Workers, of course.

Okay, perhaps. So we have one possibility offered, that it is workers—which is what Marxists themselves would answer. And we certainly know it's not capitalists. Right? Although, who was a capitalist?

Engels was.

Yes, and so not every picture is perfect. Social theory doesn't work out like astronomy or mechanics with no deviations from expectations (though Newton, you might be interested in knowing, was very much into the occult). Still, Engels should not have been a capitalist for this part of our story to flow smoothly. The fact that he was a capitalist, from our perspective, is somewhat distracting. But he was, and although capitalists are supposed to have a certain kind of worldview, he didn't fit the mold. But the mold works pretty well, most of the time, and so society has features that cause it to create groups or classes that have specific interests and look at the world in light of those interests. Bourgeois economists look at the world and formulate neoclassical economics to rationalize it. Business schools look at the world and come up with an operating framework (that actually shares many insights with Marxism, one would notice if one took the time to examine it) in order to maximize profits. And somebody else comes up with Marxism, an economic framework to try and understand the world from the point of view of a subordinate class, not the capitalists.

Okay, what about anarchism—what is anarchism? It's looking at the world from which angle? It pursues whose interest?

People's?

A citizen's?

Yes, a citizen's, that's what I would answer too. Some people would say anarchism represents the perspective of all people, but I think it is more accurate to say it represents the perspective of citizens, or, in other words, the perspective of the governed.

Of course, all the approaches we have been discussing try to broaden out and address everything at some point, at least in the hands of sensible practitioners. But if you ask about the heart of anarchism, I think it's about people as citizens as compared to governors. And opposition to the order-taker role is what breeds anarchism. And feminism is clearly about women's position and interests. And nationalism: Who are nationalists?

Usually ethnic groups?

Exactly. Racial or ethnic groups and other cultural communities often become nationalist in their approach. So there is presumably a dynamic whereby humanity is divided into contesting groups based on cultural allegiances and identity, and wherein the groups oppressed by this division begin to see this oppression as paramount and to develop a theory that highlights it.

Okay, so suppose we want to create a theory to understand societies and history. Do we want to start with people or do we want to start with something like technology, say? We have to choose.

People—what we care most about.

Alright, suppose we want to start with people at the center of our theory because people are what we care most about—the situation, prospects, and conditions of people. What kind of characteristics do we want to highlight with our concept of people? What about people do we want to pay close attention to?

Do we care about the height of people, for example? No, that's not a detail we care about as theorists of society and history, though we might care a lot about it if we were theorists of basketball, say.

Do we care about the weight of people? No, not us, though dieticians or doctors or football coaches might.

What attributes of people do we want to focus on in our intellectual framework? What do we want to highlight and pay close attention to regarding people?

The well-being of people?

Yes, of course, the well-being of people and...

Isolation between people? Power? People's desires?

People's desires and well-being, yes. And power and isolation are certainly going to come into it because we are concerned about people's individual well-being and their desires and whether or not they're fulfilled, and also about their consciousness—and clearly power and isolation affect these. And we care about these things precisely because of our interests. If we were tailors we might care more about height and girth, but we are interested in social change, so we care more about whether people are fulfilled, and we care what their consciousness is and what they're going to do about their situations. That's what we want our theory focused on.

But what do we mean by consciousness, exactly?

Some writers would take that question and do 500 pages about it, build a career on it. And that's all well and good if your intention is to delve as far into that concern as you possibly can, I guess. But that is not our aim. We want to create a broad conceptual framework, a skeletal theory that we can each fill out later as need be, given our priorities, in the areas that we pursue.

So for us consciousness doesn't demand 500 pages of complex words. Consciousness is just what's in people's heads. It's the view people have of the world. It's how people understand their place in the world. It's how people understand their interests. It's whether or not people desire to act on those understandings. That's all very important to us in terms of how people are going to interact in society and history. So those are facets that we want in our theory, and we call it consciousness.

As a little aside, interestingly enough, when we listed some concepts that were critical to the other frameworks we've discussed— anarchism, Marxism, nationalism, and feminism—there wasn't much said about human qualities. Jean-Paul Sartre, the French existentialist philosopher, who was also a Marxist and sometimes an activist, has an instructive passage where he says very critically that for Marxism a person is someone who sleeps, eats, and works. That's a slight exaggeration because many Marxists get beyond that in their thinking, of course. But if you look at the core of Marxist theory, the concept of the human being that's in that core is indeed somebody who has to live; and to live they have to eat and have a place to stay; and to have the means to eat and house themselves they have to work to gain income. Beyond that, there is not a very rich picture of humans inside the framework of Marxist economic theory, the labor theory of value, and so on. The broader attributes of what a person is aren't prioritized right at the heart of the conceptual framework.

We might ask, "What is the heart of the picture of a person in feminism?" Is it all sides of the person? What's highlighted?

Gender?

Yes. In feminist conceptualizations, sex life and procreative and household activity having to do with families in particular, are emphasized, where in contrast you can read whole volumes of Marxist economics and historical analysis and that side of life will barely be present at all.

It isn't that Marxists don't know that sex and family exist or never pay attention to it, of course. Nor am I saying that feminists don't know there is class and economy and never pay attention to it. Rather, as we will see later, each school addresses almost all things primarily from one or another angle, addressing issues other than their primary focus only secondarily and largely in terms of the impact of that primary focus.

So, yes, gender is at the heart of the feminist's concept of people. It's the aspect featured, the aspect organizing the discussion. But this is not surprising and in fact, there is nothing a priori wrong with this. Feminists are trying to understand a particular part of existence. They highlight what is likely most relevant to their agenda. That makes sense, though like anyone, they could make mistakes. The big problem will arise if they claim to understand parts of existence that they are, in fact, overlooking. Or trouble will surface also if they haven't included all that they need to include even to understand the side of life they care about.

But for now, let's continue.

What is the other really fundamental, rock-bottom thing that we need to focus on in our core concepts, in addition to people, to develop a conceptual framework to accurately analyze society and history? What else centrally composes what we call society?

The environment?

Another thing is the natural environment, to be sure. And someone might want to proceed with this theory-building process by putting the environment in the mix next. And maybe that would be a wonderful way to continue. But I don't like that step, not just yet—so what else, other than the natural environment?

Institutions?

Yes, institutions. So we know intuitively, even before we have a theory, that we need people in our theory because they're who we care most about. And we must have a view of people sufficient for what we want to be in touch with about how society and history impact people, and vice versa. But we know also that we need institutions in our conceptual tool box, because institutions compose the system that molds people and that puts constraints on us and that we have to deal with, as well as institutions being affected by people's choices, of course.

Okay, so the next question is obvious: What is an institution?

Government?

Yes, that's an institution, and it's a good idea to start to answer that way. If we can first list examples of particular institutions it may be easier to then figure out what makes each example an institution as such—what they all have in common. Government is an institution. What else?

Churches?

Labor unions?

Yes, and a school is an institution. Family is an institution.

Multinational corporation?

Yes, multinational corporation is an institution.

Boy Scouts?

Boy Scouts is an institution, yes. And what shared attributes make all these institutions? What do we mean when we say that such and such is an institution? What does this concept refer to?

And as we answer this, please realize that this is what theory-building is all about: getting a grip on some facets of reality and their key attributes and relations; defining concepts; charting their interactions and dynamics. Okay, so what is an institution?

Is it the roles people fill and the relations between them?

Well, yes, I think it is. I was hoping we'd get a lot of other answers first that we could assess, but that's good. That's, I think, the right answer.

Clearly one thing an institution is not, which someone might have answered, is its physical buildings. Of course, we sometimes think about an institution as if it is the buildings, but the Pentagon—the five-sided cement structure—isn't the institution. And it's not really the people inside the Pentagon either, though someone might have given that as a possible answer. People come and go, but still the institution called the Pentagon remains, whoever happens to be working in it. The people are critically important, of course, but they aren't themselves the institution. That's why we have people as a key concept and institution as a second key concept. The institution is something other than the people. It's the roles and the relations among the roles which people slot into. So what does that mean?

That the institution determines what we can do or be?

Exactly so. We're limited in our activities by how we fit into an available institution. Everybody who relates to some institution must fit into one place or another, into one or another slot or role that is available. So there's an institution, such as the Pentagon or the Boy Scouts, and then there is also the array of all institutions, and either we fit in some places in that whole collection and as a result we get some aspects of what institutions have to offer and do some of what institutions require, or we don't fit in it, and we get nothing. (Or we change the whole situation, but more on that later.)

So what if we want to give a name to that whole thing? In other words, we now have a concept, institution. We know that instances of this concept are all those things that people listed earlier such as school and government and Boy Scouts and many more that we could list. But what about all institutions taken together? What are we going to call that?

Society?

The state?

The infrastructure?

The system?

The state, the society, the infrastructure, the system. That last one is actually what people tend to call it in daily life. People call it "the man" also, sometimes. That is, people tend to have some vernacular colloquial phrase: the goddamn system, "they," even. But we don't really mean "they," we really mean "it." We mean the network of institutions around us that gives us choices and also limits the choices we have available. It isn't just the state, but also includes the economy and other sides of life. I like to call it the institutional boundary. It is not the state, though it includes the institutions of the state, of course. And it is not society, because it isn't the people. It isn't the infrastructure, because it isn't material things such as roads and buildings. It is the system of institutional role offerings and their relations—or the institutional boundary, in my terminology. I'm not very good with names; I'm sorry. But I like to call it the boundary, anyhow. You can call it something else, or in fact you can dispense with that concept altogether or redefine it however you choose. In other words, concepts aren't written in stone. Theories are what we make them. So, we'll call the sum of all the institutions in the society the institutional boundary, because like a boundary it constrains us. We have to fit into this institutional boundary in some place or places.

And what is your situation if you don't fit into it?

You're on the outs. You're on the bridge.

I don't know this language quite so well, but I think we agree. You're out of it. To partake in society, you're going to have to fit in some role in some institution, or more accurately into several roles in a number of institutions. Otherwise you won't be doing what the institutional boundary dictates, but you also won't be getting what it has to offer. So we now have the collection of institutions constituting the boundary. What about all the people? We have person as a concept; do we need a name for all the people as a whole?

The filler?

There you go. I agree, but I like to call the people, all together, the center—it sounds a little less like people as peanut butter. And so since I'm talking the most, and I have to remember the label, I'm going to call the sum of all the people the human center for the sake of this discussion. But we could have called it the filler or anything else we chose, of course. And what we mean by society's center (or filler) is its entire people and their levels of fulfillment and skills and knowledge and consciousness and so on, not only individually but in groups—everything that we included in our concept person for close tracking in our theory, only writ large now, covering all people.

And so now what phrase is quite similar to the new pair of concepts we've just settled on, but from another perspective? Somebody here should have a pair of concepts popping into their mind from Marxism, concepts that sound a little like human center and institutional boundary.

Totalitarianism?

The media repeats Marxism and totalitarianism in the same breath so often that it naturally pops up, but not that word, no...

Superstructure?

Yes, base/superstructure. Exactly. What is the base in Marxism? The economy. What's the superstructure? Everything else. So notice what's happening. Marxists are doing something similar to what we're doing: finding a way to divide society into two key components—and we'll come back to their choice and that similarity a little later.

For now, however, in our emerging conceptual system we have the human center composed of people with their level of consciousness, skills, and attitudes and ways of viewing the world. And then we have the institutional boundary, or role structures. This is just our way of cutting up reality to look at it and think about it. Other schools of thought will naturally cut things up differently. Our way may be effective or it may not. We'll have to see. But that's all we or any theorist can do at the basement stage of creating theory. We cut up reality, drawing a line here and there, naming the pieces. If we do this well, the features we focus on will prove useful to understanding, predicting, and intervening in society and history. If we do it poorly, we'll have to start over.

So we have human center and we have institutional boundary. And boundary is the name for the conglomeration of institutions that provide the role structures that we have to fill if we're going to be part of society. And the center is the population with their needs and desires, their level of fulfillment, and their consciousness, including skills and awareness, and particularly their political consciousness. That was our broad concept of people.

So, do we need to go any further? Is there just one big division center/boundary that we need to define to get on about the business of understanding society and history? Or are there more concepts we need to discern in the tapestry of social reality before we start looking for their connections and interrelations?

Let's enlarge on our understanding of the institutional boundary. Do we want to give a name to any key parts of it, in order to distinguish them from the whole thing? You see what I'm saying? Someone give me an example of a name that could demarcate part of the whole institutional boundary, not just a single institution, but a subset of the whole.

The economy?

Exactly right. We could name a part of the institutional boundary, for example, the economy. Could we give a name to some other part of it?

Patriarchy?

Patriarchy, but patriarchy is a concept like capitalism is a concept, instead of like the economy is a concept. It's not an instance of a part of the boundary of society, but a particular type of instance. What's it a type of? If capitalism is a specific type of economy, then similarly what is patriarchy a specific type of?

Power structure?

Oppression?

Sometimes you have concepts already in mind; sometimes it takes a little more pushing and pulling to come up with something that will be useful. What's the part of the reality that can be patriarchal, or better, what's the seat of patriarchy, the origin point of it?

The family?

Yes, we can call it the kinship sphere or some label like that to be a bit broader than one single institution—just as we have the concept economy rather than factory. In other words, here we have another part of the institutional boundary that we can carve off as a separate concept, the kinship sphere. And the kinship sphere can be patriarchal or not, just as the economy can be capitalist or not.

What's another part of the boundary that's going to be more obvious now that we've done this much? (As we do it, I think things will become clearer.)

The government, the state?

Yes. The political apparatus or whatever you want to call it. What's another one?

Culture?

Yes, culture. Now someone may come up with more aspects to focus on in the boundary, finding more key parts of it to label that we want to pay special attention to. But I'm going to stop finding parts for a moment. I think we're doing pretty well already. Frugality is key to the art of building good theory. Don't create more concepts than you need, but do create enough concepts to be sufficient for your needs.

It seems to me that if we look at society's institutional boundary we can see that there are different parts of it that are each powerfully important. We want to put a label on them so we can pay close attention to each of them in our theorizing. We want to highlight them so we can see how they move and change and how they impact one another and people, rather than only highlighting the whole institutional boundary, and not differentiating these subsystems within it.

The economy, kinship sphere, polity, and the cultural sphere or community sphere—whatever you want to call them—they're what I see when I look at society. All four exist in our society, clearly. But do they exist in every society? We're building a theory; are these concepts always applicable?

Is there ever a society that doesn't have an economy? Is there ever a society that doesn't have a kinship sphere? Is there ever a society that doesn't have a cultural sphere? Is there ever a society that doesn't have some kind of polity, some kind of political coordination of decisions? No, I don't think so. I think all four are always present.

But why?

Because each of these spheres of social life has a function that defines it, and that function has to be achieved in any society. So it becomes clear that we have additional concepts entering our tool box. And, indeed, this is the way to build concepts and theory, slowly but surely.

3. More Concepts and the Utility of Social Theory

New opinions are always suspected and usually opposed without any other reason but because they are not already common.

–John Locke

Most everybody I see knows the truth but they just don't know that they know it.

–Woody Guthrie

Polity, economy, kinship, and culture or community—we had begun asking why these divisions exist. Why do we care about them? What functions does each have?

What about the economy? What functions are carried out in the economy?

Exchange and consumption?

Yes, and you also have to produce, so together production, allocation among people, and consumption constitute economies. Correct.

What about the kinship sphere? What function does it accomplish?

Socialization?

Socialization. Yes, and what is socialized?

People.

Yes, children born through procreation, as they inevitably are. So it's procreation and socialization, and it's everything going into these, including courtship, etc. So gender roles and relations, sex, and procreation and socialization are the functions that give rise to kinship institutions.

All of this, by the way, isn't written in stone. You could start over again an hour from now and come up with something different. That's what theories are. There isn't one theory of the world. Theory is the process of taking the world apart, putting it into concepts, and figuring out their interrelations. Then maybe you have something that's accurate and that explains some part of existence usefully, something revealing that can predict or guide.

For instance, in our earlier example, you had a theory of the radio and I had a theory of the radio. Mine is basic: turn the knob, sound flows. But you are an electrician and so you unscrew the case and poke around in there and make it do things, and so you have all sorts of concepts I don't have—diodes and other things inside. My purpose is to hear the music. Your purpose is to correct operating problems. You have a different theory of the exact same thing, the radio.

It's the same with the world more broadly. You can have lots of different theories of parts of the world or even of the whole world, though taken in different ways and highlighting different facets, because you can have a lot of different purposes. The commonality is that each conceptualization has to stand the test of accuracy. You can't just make up whatever you like. You play close attention to whatever you choose, as long as you are truthful and your concepts correspond to reality, and help you understand, predict, and intervene.

Okay, so what's the function that generates community or cultural institutions? What's the function at the basis of creating that sphere of life?

Identity?

I think so too, but it took me years to get to that, and it apparently took you about fifteen seconds. I'm impressed. In any case, we have identity, some kind of identification and celebration—this seems to be at the heart of culture.

Now, a question arises: Why do these functions have to be fulfilled?

But first we might ask, "How do you answer questions like this as they arise in your conceptualizing some subject area?" Well, you first try to do it using the conceptual apparatus that you are developing, using what you already have in hand. If you can do that, that's great. If you can't do that and the question is important to you, then that's a warning that you need to change or add concepts. That's how you refine theory. We may need to create another concept to answer our question. We may not have enough concepts yet. However, I think we do have enough, broadly. So why do these functions have to be achieved?

Society produces itself?

Well, that sounds interesting, but so far we don't even have a very clear and full concept "society," so while your answer is interesting, it isn't something we are able to even say, as yet, supposing we are working within our emerging framework. So using just what we have, what is it that causes there to necessarily be production and allocation, procreation and socialization, identification and celebration, and coordination of decision-making, implementation of shared projects, and adjudication?

Well, the only thing we have is people.

Yes, exactly, people with certain needs and desires and capabilities. And we have the concept of the human center—so we have to see if that's where the answer resides. Is it something about people per se that requires that these functions have to be carried out?

Sure, we can't live and especially live well without them.

Yes. And don't be alarmed that it seems so simple. It is supposed to seem simple. It is good if it seems simple. That's what good theory does: it makes generating useful insights simple. We haven't gotten there yet, but we're getting close. Our goal isn't to make things complex, but to have a framework that makes things evident and easy, that pushes us to insights with little effort.

So sure, that's the answer, and you could imagine people who were different from us such that these functions didn't have to happen as they do for us. For instance, you could imagine a one-gender species in which procreation was automatic and each new child was born whole and adult upon arrival, so there were no significant relations involved in that domain at all. That would get rid of one of those four sets of institutions by eliminating the function those institutions fulfill. And in fact not all species have procreation and socialization the way we do, so maybe there are some sentient species somewhere in the universe that don't require social institutions with role structures to get the kinship job done, so their worlds don't have institutions being created and a whole sphere of social life emerging to fulfill these functions. In other words, it's the innate characteristics of human beings that are at work in making the functions we have identified require institutions to get them done in human societies. Literally what we are and what our nature is makes it inevitable that these four types of functions and the institutions to accomplish them will exist in human societies. The functions don't exist because Newton's Laws make them exist. And they exist neither because a sociologist made them exist, nor a special history that is unique to our country alone made them exist. They exist for all people, everywhere, all the time, because of who we are. We need them. These functions have to be fulfilled because human beings require it.

So suppose we were going to already ask about how to theorize a society. What would be the guess? What would you do at this stage? What would it mean?

Wait, what is the function of polity?

Hmm, you are right, I jumped ahead of myself. I apologize. Well, I think the function is broadly the accommodation of differing wills. If you have lots of people and they have diverse inclinations— sometimes contrary inclinations and sometimes even inclinations that seriously clash—still, you have to somehow accommodate it all. That's what the polity is about. You can go further into its components; accommodation occurs regarding legislating laws or rules, regarding implementing shared aims, and regarding adjudicating disputes or violations of norms. And, in fact, that's the point I was getting at next. You can take each of these spheres of institutions and develop additional concepts that are suitable to comprehending that sphere in more detail, and in that way you begin to theorize further. Notice also, that if we have some concepts about the economy and we have some concepts about the polity, we might need to do something further. We're going to have to look at how they relate to each other and to come up with some concepts to address that interrelationship, no doubt.

Does it seem as though we're leaving something fundamental out? It could. We have people. We have the totality of institutions. We have basic critical parts of that institutional whole deriving from the character of humans and their intrinsic requirements. So we have to consider whether we think that at this basic level we are missing anything critical. Or whether we are highlighting things in a way that overemphasizes lowly matters and underemphasizes more critical aspects, for example.

What did you say was missing, earlier?

Environment?

Yes. Is environment missing? Should we have it as a concept?

I think it needs to be included, but by your definition of institutions being those things where you have people fulfilling roles, the environment doesn't seem to have a conceptual place.

And that's an excellent point. Look what's happening. We started picking out concepts and the concepts are already affecting how we see the world and what other concepts we in turn define. That's what concepts do. That's what a theory does. A theory is a little like a pair of tinted glasses. You put on the tinted glasses and if they're red, everything's tinted red. If they're green, everything's tinted green. Similarly, theories contour our view of reality and make it easier to see some aspects than others, to be more attuned or more aware of some features than others. We see reality through our concepts and so we see what our concepts emphasize but don't see what they leave out.

So you're right. We put our initial emphasis on institutions and specifically on roles that people fill, and on the people themselves. And so we're barreling along with that mindset, and what's missing? The environment is missing because it's neither part of the institutional boundary nor of the human center. That's correct. And that's exactly why it was missing, I think, at this point in the process the first time this process was done by Robin Hahnel and myself. We were barreling along, but unlike you, we had personal agendas and priorities at that time that were not particularly ecological, and so we didn't pause right here and say, "Hold on, we left something out." For a time, at least, we just proceeded and only later realized that perhaps we had a bit of a hole in the framework. And we might've made a big mistake had we not noticed the absence at all, or had we become so enamored of our concepts and their lessons and relations that later, when told, "Hey, you don't have the environment at a basic level," we had dismissively replied, "Well, no, we don't but that's because it isn't basic; it is derivative." We might've barreled ahead, in other words, filled up our conceptual tool box and left out something very important or might have later relegated it to a position of relative unimportance incongruous with how the world really is. That's what happens, actually, quite often, in theory building. That's what happens, for example, with all four of the conceptual frameworks (anarchism, Marxism, nationalism, and feminism) that we have mentioned. They each get a lot right, to be sure, but they also leave out important aspects, given their priorities or biases, and they don't adequately correct for it later. And perhaps we'll make that error too, but at least we know what they left out, so perhaps we can do somewhat better than they did. Anyway, getting back to our project, if we have the human center and the institutional boundary—what is the environment?

Another sphere?

Well, we already used that term for dimensions of social life— that is, for domains of institutions with essential social functions. That doesn't sound like the environment to me. It isn't a domain of institutions. It doesn't exist to fulfill social functions for people. We've come up with the idea of a sphere of social life and we have four of those, each existing to fulfill functions required by human needs. But what would the environment be seen as, in that light? It doesn't work to classify it that way. It is something important, but it is something different.

There is the environment, not on our conceptual list so far, and then we might as well note now, there is also the rest of the world— also not in our list so far. So far we have been talking about a society, one society. But what about all the other societies?

In a sense, each society is in a context. And the context is most broadly the environment on the one hand, and the rest of the world of other societies, on the other hand. This conceptual selection is one way of organizing the components that we carve out of the whole reality. If you come up with a different way to do it, that's fine. If it helps you explain, predict, and guide, that's excellent. But we started with society, with key aspects of it, and we are now going to enmesh it with ecology and international relations. Someone else might have started with nature, or perhaps with the world, and discerned society later, as a part of the whole—as we started with the institutional boundary and then found economy, polity, etc., rather than the reverse order.

Or perhaps someone else using a different path would arrive at entirely different slices of reality to highlight via different concepts. So how do we know which way of defining concepts and of later determining their interrelations we prefer? It depends on what we need to explain, predict, or guide. It depends on who is going to use the conceptual tool box and for what purpose. Which way of cutting up reality into truthful concepts helps us most? Beyond requiring accuracy, that's the way we ought to choose.

So we are trying to make a theory that will allow us to understand society and history. Have we said anything about history yet? No, because we haven't incorporated change. We have no dynamics. We have no concepts relating to change, and that's what history is: change over time. We don't even have time yet, as a matter of fact. So far we're only looking at a snapshot of society and trying to pick out what matters at a single moment. We're looking at society, but of course there are really lots of societies. So there's international relations as well, as soon as we recognize that each society is set in the context of the whole array of all other societies. It's almost like a second boundary—this time a new, larger, different type of boundary for the combination of any particular society's institutional boundary and human center. It's a context they operate within and, for that matter that they affect and thus contribute to. And another part of that surrounding context would be the environment. The environment or ecology is a kind of setting or stage on which the whole society is acted. Does seeing the ecology and international relations as the setting for society make them more important? Less important? It doesn't really do either. The environment and international relations are critical, we can agree on that much, and so we need to include them in our conceptual framework, and this is a way to do it.

But if we return to the concepts we are developing, where do we put that? You say people are the center and there's an institutional boundary and the boundary seems somehow visually huge to me in comparison to the center. And now there's the environment; it's even bigger.

Well, that's one way to think about this pictorially. But somebody else might envision a huge human center, say the whole inside of a sphere including all these people in their many facets and various groupings, and then see a thin institutional boundary as a kind of surface shell surrounding this big solid spherical center. And maybe they see the whole sphere adrift in a sea of ecology and other societies. I would imagine we could picture these concepts in several ways, and each way might tend to propel us in a slightly different conceptual direction. But then hopefully by demanding that our concepts be true to reality, as well as useful, the way we each visually picture it will come into accord with what others using slightly different imagery come up with. If you want to see a book that pictures these types of concepts in some diagrams, get a copy of *Liberating Theory* by myself, Noam Chomsky, Holly Sklar, Lydia Sargent, Robin Hahnel, Mel King and Leslie Cagan. There are diagrams in that book that show how we pictured this theory while we were writing the book, or more accurately, at the moment of drawing. But be warned, many readers just burst into laughter when they see the pictures, unimpressed with our graphic sense.

Okay now I'm into a visual image of it: of the institutions, of the boundary surrounding all the people. It has no contact with the people it is just penning them in.

First, we don't have finished concepts, yet. Theorizing is the work of developing and refining and adapting concepts. So you don't want to settle on too complete an image too early in the game. You want to be flexible, so that you can alter your views in response to accumulating evidence and further thought, plus the experience of using them and seeing how they work out in practice. That said, for your visualization, what is the actual contact between center and boundary as we have so far conceived them?

Well, people fill the role slots that the boundary creates. And on the other hand, the institutions of the boundary exist because people need certain functions fulfilled and create institutions to accomplish them—in time, also altering those institutions in various ways that we haven't yet discussed. The boundary affects who we are and we in turn impact what the boundary's features are. The boundary limits and constrains us in ways we'll see shortly. People guarantee that the boundary has certain components, and beyond that, people may alter other components.

So how do we find people as different from one another, rather than just being similar cogs in a big machine?

People aren't simply derivative parts of institutions in our unfolding conceptualization, entirely generated by institutions cookie cutter–like, as if we were formed in some mold that institutions enforce on us. People are genetically endowed. We are biological entities. Sure, if we each live in proximity to different institutional boundaries we will grow up to act differently than one another. In fitting into institutional roles we develop new levels of fulfillment, new agendas and consciousness, or new suffering, because of the implications the roles have for our lives and choices. But people are not homogenous. We are diverse, very varied, though molded and pressured by overarching institutions that impact even different people similarly.

But when you call it a boundary—I mean, you could also call it a structure—you're interested only in the limit of it. That's why you call it a boundary.

Well, mostly I come up with the names due to the poverty of my imagination. But I don't want that name boundary to give a wrong impression. It places limits on people's options, yes, but it also allows people to accomplish otherwise impossible things. I should make that clear. The whole point was that there were functions in society that need to get done by virtue of the nature of people, and in dealing with these functions various institutions evolved. So these institutions don't just place limits on people. Our institutional modes of procreation and socialization aren't just boundaries, they aren't just limitations— they're also positive facilitators. Our modes of production and allocation offer possibilities, not just limitations. These functions and the institutions devoted to accomplishing them exist because we require them. If we didn't have institutions for these functions, we couldn't live. The institutions that fulfill these functions permit us certain options, but also limit others. They may be allowing life for many, yet limiting life's options at the same time, for some. We may require the function, but not enjoy the mode by which it is currently accomplished, though that jumps ahead of where we are in our conceptualizing.

For now, however, why do these particular functions get our attention? Why do we conceptually identify these functions? Why do we hone in on them? What about breathing, for example? How come I didn't identify breathing as a critical function?

We just do it. There aren't different alternatives for breathing.

Fair enough. But also, it doesn't yield a set of institutions that has powerful effects on our personalities, on our possibilities, on our fulfillment and achievements—on the things we want our theory to help us understand.

But what if I said thinking was actually a critical function? Maybe someone wants to come along and re-conceptualize our four spheres by noting that thinking is always present in human societies, owing to the nature of humans, just as seeking identity, or producing and consuming, or accommodating wills, or procreating and socializing are always present in human societies owing to our nature. The person might argue for trying to discern associated structures or institutions that make up a new sphere of life relating to thinking as a defining function. I don't intuit its importance nor do I want to explore it. But someone else might intuit its importance, and want to explore it, feeling that it is a possible key addition to their conceptualization. And so they might come up with a fifth sphere, and it might help practitioners using their conceptual framework to see important and relevant truths about societies and about history more fully or more accurately than my four sphere approach does. If that happens, I should change my views. But for now, I have reason to think the four spheres are highly and usefully correlated to radical needs, so I want to continue pursuing them and see where it takes us. That's what theorizing is all about. If our concepts take us to a place where we are stuck, then we have to go back and refine them, or maybe we have to eliminate something wrong, or add something new, or perhaps even start over. We'll see.

What is your view of human nature?

That's a separate issue, it takes us a bit off our path, but lots of people feel confused about this question in their own thinking, so let me try to answer it quickly, even at the risk of a slight departure from schedule.

First, I should say that I think it's a very serious question for leftists concerned about changing the world for the better. I think when you go out organizing, if you are a good organizer and you work hard at communicating with people, you are often going to get to the point where people say to you, "But human nature sucks and therefore the world is going to always suck, so stop wasting my time."

I tell those people that I don't feel that way at all. I tell them that I think human nature is, in fact, very variegated. It obviously allows for anti-social behavior or even serial murder, for that matter. This isn't an open question. We know that human nature is compatible with people doing all sorts of bad things because such things have in fact happened. In other words, in the range of all the things that human nature makes possible, surely we will find at least all the things that humans have already done. So human nature plus complicated circumstances can yield anti-social behavior, and even serial murder. Indeed, it has done so.

But it seems to me that human nature can also manifest all the positive values we espouse. So how do we respond to somebody who says that people are evil and greedy, at their root, and that greediness is an inevitable outgrowth in all social situations? Of course we might start by asking if the person himself is greedy and evil, or if she thinks we are, and so on; but beyond that I might confront him with an argument Noam Chomsky originated and likes to use. I say to the person, "Consider someone walking down the street and there is a little child with an ice cream cone and it's a really hot day. It's just horribly hot out and the child has an ice cream cone and the person walking down the street is an adult and is really hungry and hot. There is nobody around but the two of them. Does the adult take the ice cream cone, brush the child into the gutter, and walk on?"

After they finish chuckling or frowning at the scenario, I then ask, "Okay, if that isn't your expectation for the average adult's behavior, what do we say about a person who does do that? Suppose you were up in a window overlooking the street and you saw someone take the cone, smack the kid into the gutter, and walk off." Most people I try this with will say that there is something wrong with this bully. The bully's wiring is out of whack. I need only then point out that to think this about the adult taking the ice cream cone assumes at heart that this bullying adult is in some way pathological, deviating from what it is to be a normal person.

And now we have a conundrum. This cynic from our example on the one hand thinks humans are inevitably so evil and greedy that these traits will always characterize and even dominate any human society. But when asked about this ice cream cone example and the evil and greedy behavior embedded in it, the person all of a sudden thinks it's pathological to behave this way. First, evil propensities are the norm for humanity, when saying so wards off the responsibility of making the world a better place. Then the same or even lesser evil propensities are pathological when actual situations are looked at and there is no implication for life choices at stake. The point may or may not register.

There's another response that I like. People will say, "Well the world is so horrible that it must be human nature that causes it. There is evil everywhere, so it is just the nature of things stemming from us." And I reply that oddly my feeling is the exact opposite: "It seems to me that if I can find one person who behaves consonant with what I call goodness—I don't care who it is, Che Guevara or your aunt, a friend or some saint, it doesn't matter—that is better evidence that human nature is good than all the easy to find bad people in history are evidence for the counter view." Why do I say this?

The relevant insight is that the institutional boundary that we've had since the beginning of recorded history has always had role slots that produce anti-social behavior. So everything around us has pushed for the horrible outcomes we endure. The fact that we have greed and war and other vulgarity is easily explained as an outgrowth of the pressures of those institutions. In fact, if you look at the preponderance of those institutions, you have to ask yourself the opposite question: Where does good behavior come from? In other words, it is harder to find the origin for sociality and justice and equity and for being fair, which, however, anyone will certainly admit do exist around us. Where do they come from? Anti-social behavior is propelled by the institutions and is easy to explain. What about a nice person? It's hard to explain "niceness" because everything about the social structure around us pushes us toward competing and grabbing. So that's why I think that if you identify one nice person—

whether it's your aunt, your uncle, or yourself—that's good evidence on behalf of social rather than anti-social natural human inclinations.

Maybe it will turn out that we need to have a far richer description of people based on volumes of psychological studies, or whatever. I doubt it, though. For now we can each have our view of what humans are and how they act, as long as our view includes that we have various innate facets and that these interact with the circumstances we encounter to determine our levels of fulfillment and consciousness and skills and so on—and as long as we believe that in that interplay it is not only possible that people will be anti-social and greedy, but also possible that people will be social and empathetic. In that case, we agree enough to proceed. Concepts will be elaborated upon and filled out by proceeding with using them, one step at a time. So, for now let's proceed with a step that follows the sequence we have been pursuing and that might take us forward.

Please name some societies in the world, some countries in the world and let's see if we can do anything with the conceptual map we already have in hand.

Sweden. Ireland.

We are going to have to name some more. Name ones that are exemplars of types in your mind, if you can.

South Africa ... the Soviet Union.

Okay, how can we apply our theory to these different countries? Well, with our theory we can explore a lot of facets when we first look at a country. We can ask about a state of consciousness and fulfillment at the human center: What is the state of skill development? And about the institutional boundary, we can ask, "What are the institutional structures of the economy, polity, cultural sphere, and kinship sphere?"

Suppose we are following such a path and we ask whether South Africa and the United States are the same kind of society. Suppose we ask that question and we are Marxist in our approach. What's our answer for South Africa and the United States both twenty years ago?

Yes, they are the same.

If we're a Marxist the answer is yes; we'd say that they are the same kind of country. That's correct. Why is that the case?

They are both capitalist.

Yes, and that's the end of the issue, because for the Marxist the economy is the defining feature. If the economy is the same type for two countries, then the societies are the same type between those two. They both have capitalist economies and so they are the same kind of society. But do we agree with this? How many people think they're not the same type of society, that there's something fundamentally different?

Turns out nearly everyone does. Okay, let's continue with the survey. How does the Marxist compare the United States and the Soviet Union, twenty years ago, say?

They're different.

"They are different," says the Marxist. And why?

Well, because the economies are different, of course.

But who would suggest that South Africa and the United States were different in as fundamental and important a way as the Soviet Union and the United States were different? Does any perspective lead to that viewpoint? Which theorist thinks that?

A nationalist?

See how easy this is? Yes, the nationalist might not only look at South Africa and the U.S. twenty years ago and say they are profoundly different, but he or she might also look at the Soviet Union and the United States and say they aren't much different. If our understanding of the world says that those four spheres are all really important and decisive in defining the nature of society—and we haven't offered much reason to believe that yet—then if we have two societies in which one of these spheres is systematically different than in the other, we have two different kinds of societies. That would be what our concepts are pointing toward. That's what our concepts would be telling us.

The point is, it's our theory—or the theory of the nationalist or the Marxist or whoever—that gives us each our respective opinion about how much the differences we see (and everyone sees some differences) matter.

So Marxists see a big difference between the Soviet Union and the United States, but many feminists emphasizing kinship and gender don't see such a difference between those two countries. They say that both societies are patriarchal and we should just get on with the business of dealing with that. And they then may even get a bit angry at someone saying that these two societies are hugely different because regarding the attributes that feminists highlight, the two societies don't seem to be that different. And then the Marxist may strike back by noting that a lot of women are doctors in the Soviet Union. And what does a really sharp feminist deduce from that?

That the status of the doctors in the Soviet Union is low?

Yes, and this is where theory starts to be powerful. If you've got a theory that tells you certain things, it will help you make certain predictions— and indeed your answer was an example of using a theory to make a prediction.

In other words, we look and see that the Soviet Union is patriarchal. What does our theory tell us will be true if a society is patriarchal? It says there will be a sexist division of labor and a sexist division of virtually all social roles, for that matter, and women will generally be subordinate.

Now, we look further and we see, or we are told by the Marxist, that women are disproportionately filling this slot called doctor which has in our experience a lot of status, income, and power. But wait a minute. How could the society be sexist if most doctors are women? There isn't a big women's movement forcing that outcome—it is just the norm?

Well we can deduce something. Either the society's not sexist in the way that we understand sexism or being a doctor actually isn't all that cool. And you deduced that being a doctor wasn't all that cool. That's what a theory is all about. A theory is good if it can tell you something beyond the specific facts you have at hand. Of course, whether all this is true or not, one ultimately has to investigate to see. Maybe other factors complicate the situation. Maybe there is some struggle and unstable situation, as we'll understand shortly. It is the method, the reasoning, that I want to get across.

Okay. Now suppose we ask what a revolution is. We'll just try to quickly begin to address some concepts we are going to deal with more in coming chapters, because part of the logic we'll use there stems from what we discussed immediately above. What is the concept of revolution? What does revolution mean?

Change in the system.

Change in the system? What system are we talking about here? What we're doing is we're theorizing a society, so if revolution were a change in the system, in this case, the system would be a society. So what else?

Reordering of the roles and the relationships?

Now here is someone trying to use the theory we are developing. He is saying, "What are our concepts? Now if we can't define revolution in the context of the concepts we have, then maybe we need something new, but we ought to try doing it with what we have first." And in the context of what we've got, what is it?

It's a reordering of roles and relationships.

Which ones?

Of the institutions?

Yes, but is it just any reordering of any institutions? We could of course define it that way, because a concept is something we define. We can make it anything we want. But what's useful for us?

That it be more about the spheres?

I would say it should take into account all of the spheres.

It's what's important to you—maybe if you're a patriarch you don't want to change the kinship roles, but if you're a worker, you may want a revolution based on that relationship but not the other relationships.

It's a question of how we are going to label to things. And this question is important because how we label things—the concepts that we establish—affects whether anyone who has different backgrounds and interests than we do is going to relate to our theory, and also whether our concepts are going to direct attention in useful ways.

One possibility is that we could define the word revolution to mean a change in which the defining features (and we haven't yet said anything to indicate what features are defining and what features are less critical) of each of the four spheres have changed. So all four of the spheres have to have their defining features changed for there to be a revolution. Suppose we define revolution that way. Somebody tell me a revolution that has occurred.

But then there is no revolution in Eastern Europe. There was none in South Africa.

Yes, if you choose this definition you would have to say precisely that. But there are a lot of people who will disagree with that. On the other hand, will everybody say that there was a revolution in South Africa when apartheid was eliminated?

No.

Who won't?

The economists?

Well, yes, the Marxists won't call that a revolution. And they have a point. It's still a capitalist economy and many things are the same as before. And the constraints capitalist institutions impose are very powerful. All that said, do we want to call it a revolution?

It was a major change...

Yes, it was a major change in the defining relations in one of the four spheres that we have highlighted. So what definition of the word revolution is going to be most useful to us given that the operational value of the theory is always at stake in such choices, as well as its accuracy? In fact, maybe we should just take a minute to explore that point further.

Suppose we ask about a social theory what attributes it needs to have to be useful to us in working to make the world a better place. We know it has to explain. We know is has to predict. We know it has to be useful for guidance. Are there any other qualities it needs to have?

It has to improve things.

Well the people using it are the ones improving things. But the theory has to be useful for that end, yes. Is there another quality it needs to have to be useful to that end?

It has to easily translate into practice?

What does that mean: "It has to easily translate into practice"? Who is going to use it? Whose practice? It's an interesting suggestion. What are the possible answers? Who could use it?

Revolutionaries. People who hold the theory?

But who could that be? That could be everybody, or it could be...

It could be intellectuals.

Yes. It could be that in order to use the theory you have to sit in a library, close all the doors, shut all the noise off, think for forty-seven days, converse with somebody else who has done the same thing, for just as long or longer, and maybe come up with a result. I'm serious about this. It could be that you need a few years to learn this theory, and then each time you use it, you have to give tremendous focus and lots of time as well. In other words, we can develop a theory that is hard to learn and hard to use. Now if we do that what's going to happen?

Only experts will be able to use it.

Yes, and that's not so bad if it's a theory of the inner workings of a computer, is it? The people who are concerned with maintaining computers, if necessary, can go to school to become equipped and when they are working on the computer they can do so in a nice quiet environment, with someone else equally trained, and so on. The fact that a social theory is structured in such a way that you have to spend years learning the concepts, and then still longer learning how to think with the concepts, could be a problem, however. It might be nicer if every theory was quick to learn, but it's not a social disaster if a theory of computers or chemical combinations is hard to learn. But what if our political theory, the one meant to guide our efforts at social change, has those same attributes?

It will fail.

It will fail at what?

At transforming the larger society?

I don't see why. Perhaps this difficult theory is powerful and can discern important truths and guide people to effective actions.

But most people won't be able to participate in using it.

Why not? Because they're dumb?

No. Because it is incomprehensible. They haven't had time to learn it.

Correct, most people don't have the time. People don't have the circumstances. Which people will have the time and the circumstances?

Intellectuals.

Yes, people who are professionals at it. Exactly.

So if we create a theory that is very obtuse and very hard to use because people have to really work long and hard to get anything out of it, then we can be sure that social theorizing will be done by a relatively small circle of people. And then, once they see the light, they will pronounce their results to everybody else. If we don't want that, we'd better not construct our theory that way.

I think this argument condemns a lot of social theory that purports to be about making the world a better place, and especially about making it more participatory and democratic.

If our purpose is to understand in the library, it doesn't matter so much that our framework is difficult to use. But if our purpose is to create a tool to be utilized by people who are suffering oppression in dealing with their life situations and choices, the tool has to be user-friendly. This is straightforward and simple, a bottom-line requirement, a deal breaker—and yet it is not often said.

If Marxism-Leninism is a theory that you have to spend ages learning or, worse, if postmodernism is incomprehensible short of intense study, then it won't facilitate a participatory and public movement. If these approaches are supposed to be tools to make the world a better and particularly a more democratic and participatory place—well, you just have to be kidding. Unless of course, you believe that the right way to make the world a better place is to have a relatively small number of people utilize the concepts and figure everything out and tell everybody else what to do. But what's that approach often called?

Totalitarianism?

Well, okay, or more precisely Leninism. That's Leninist strategy, vanguard strategy. But we'll get to that in a bit.

Is there a possibility that a theory wouldn't—I don't know, I'm trying to think this through—be comprehensive and thorough enough if it were made simple enough to be popularly useful? The level of complexity of the topic is just too great to allow it to be straightforward?

Sure it's possible. In fact it is true for quantum mechanics. It is true of theories of electrons and quarks, say. And it is true for theories of microbiology. And it could be that some area of social life is so complicated that you can't understand it or make predictions about it or guide practice bearing on it at the levels necessary to help activists create worthwhile social change unless you are using a theory that is so complex that it takes a whole lot of time to learn as well as a quiet place to use.

It's possible that facets of social life are so complex that we can't make a conceptual framework user-friendly and also comprehensive enough for our purposes. Yes, that's conceivable. But the odd truth is that society is in fact so amazingly complex that to get anywhere with it at all you have to work at a rather elementary and broad level. Broad and general insights are actually all that we can confidently attain. And in fact those are not so hard to work with. And given our social priorities, we have to try very hard to generate an approach that is useable and that fits into people's available time and circumstances, before we give up such an undertaking. We have to try to do that because the cost of doing otherwise, in terms of lack of participation and imposition of elite hierarchy, is so great. Also, we need a framework that's use isn't contrary to but instead fits people's experience. Indeed, this is a more subtle point about the qualities we ought to look for in a social theory, which is also very important in thinking about what should characterize a good social theory for activists trying to improve the world. Suppose you live in a society in which there are certain harmful traits. What are some of the traits that are harmful in our society—traits we have by virtue of living here?

Greed...racism.

Yes. Racism, sexism, classism, authoritarianism, and so on. Okay, so what if your theory is constructed in such a way that if you have those attributes in your personality and in your consciousness and you try to use the theory, you will inevitably fail miserably with it?

Do you see what I'm saying? What if a theory, instead of countering those ills at the core of our suppositions and thoughts, and even leading people with those inclinations to contrary and useful insights against the impact of their biases, rather needs to be used by a perfect human being to work well? Is that desirable?

The idea is, you can have a way of conceptualizing and thinking about the world that acts against the biases we have, or you can have a way that easily falls prey to being distorted by those biases, even though it could yield great results if we had no such biases. You can have a theory that pressures a man, or a member of a dominant cultural community, say, to pay attention to the things that a man or a culturally dominant person might not pay attention to. Or you can have a theory that is such that only if you are already the perfect human being will you take into account everything you ought to highlight. If you are not so perfect, which is true for all of us, you will be easily diverted from truthful perception by your prior biases.

The fact that a theory will give great results when used by perfect people in calm settings after great training is not germane to creating a theory for participatory, democratic social change. The decisive question is of what kind of results it will yield being used by real people, in real settings, after plausible preparation.

Now, I came to believe, based on my experience of Marxism, feminism, nationalism, and anarchism many decades ago, that ideally with each one of these frameworks practitioners can arrive at very insightful results. You can come at society initially from the direction of economics or polity or gender or nationalism, and you can work with a tool box emphasizing one or the other of these angles of approach, and yet you can come to an overarching and comprehensive, powerful and compelling picture. But you could do this with any of these tool boxes, I decided, only if you were a nearly perfect human being and had lots of time and a calm environment in which to pursue your thoughts. Because each of the frameworks rather than pushing you hard to a whole conception that embodies elements that you wouldn't otherwise prioritize, instead easily succumbs to our tendencies to stop short of seeing everything important.

And so what usually happens with these conceptual frameworks instead of people arriving at a full perception of reality?

We get a narrow picture.

And it not only starts out narrow, but it doesn't successfully broaden out. Why? Because the perceptual weaknesses that we all have of not being able to see all sides of reality equally well given our limited personal backgrounds and prejudices, or even our tendency to leave out stuff that conflicts with our interests, are not countered by but are instead intensified by the theory's structure. The theory itself tends to aggravate our tendencies to be myopic, or at least it doesn't counter these weaknesses. But a good theory should counter our biases. A good social theory should work against the weaknesses of the people who are trying to employ it.

Countering our socially induced biases is an feature we need to try to consciously build into a social theory to the extent we're serious about real people in real conditions using the theory to help guide effective practice. An intellectual framework that's going to provide a useable way of looking at and thinking about the world, of trying to predict and guide radical actions, needs to be comprehensible and usable without a tremendous amount of invested time and energy. And it also has to counter our narrow-mindedness, our tendency to leave out important things. That is another kind of pressure that I feel when I sit down and try to figure out what kind of political framework would be good for each person to have in order for us to be able to collectively advance. Instead of thinking about how big the words can be, which I think is perhaps the criterion employed in the creation of postmodernism, I think about the framework having to be useable by real people in demanding circumstances.

At any rate, let's get back on track now—I'm sorry for the diversions. If we want to further elaborate what we're doing conceptually, what should we do next?

First we would enrich our concepts. We'd like to add additional concepts for each of the four spheres. We'd like to add concepts that highlight how the four spheres interact with each other and what their interrelations can be. We'd also like to develop a picture of society not only as a static snapshot, but also as it changes—and thus a picture of what revolution and social change and evolution are. And then we'd like to address how we go from our overall understanding of society now to some kind of vision of what we want and how we envision attaining that vision. And that's the overall process of developing our framework, and it is what we will address in coming chapters.

But now, to recap, we have the social center: humans and their attributes. We have the institutional boundary: institutions and their role structures that people fill. You fill the role, you have to carry out the behavior patterns that are associated with the role. Carrying out those behavior patterns affects you and your levels of fulfillment and consciousness and so on. So we've got mother, father; capitalist, worker; I don't know the names of roles in religions, but, you know, believer, priest—or member of another community, Latino, Asian, whatever it happens to be in the community you're in; and finally, citizen, governor. As you fill those roles, and refined variants of each, you carry out the required behaviors. And of course you fill many slots in each of the four spheres.

So what more do we need? We need new concepts that help us see how the spheres interact. We need concepts that help point us toward how in actual societies the four spheres pressure and mold and even define one another.

But let's do one more thing before we end this chapter and move on to thinking about how change occurs. We had a picture of society with a human center, and an institutional boundary, and the boundary's four spheres. What's the Marxist picture of society at the same level of broad definition?

Base/superstructure?

And what's the base?

The economy or as they call it, the mode of production.

Yes, the mode of production. So they say the base is the mode of production. It could be capitalism; it could be feudalism; it could be socialism. The base is the economy, right? And then the superstructure is what?

Politics...culture...sexuality?

It's everything else, yes. And so what are the Marxists saying? They are saying that economics is more basic in some sense. That's why they call it the base. They are saying if we understand the economy, we are well on our way to understanding everything. It doesn't mean they think the rest is irrelevant. But it does mean that they feel that when you understand the economic base, you understand the first-order influences, the primary aspects. The economic base manifests itself throughout the rest of society and by focusing on the economy and its class implications, you will comprehend what is most important about other facets of society too. Class pressures contour the way culture is, and the way kinship is, and the way sexuality is, and the way the state is. Is that much true?

Not necessarily.

Is it true?

No.

Hmmm.... I guess I don't always get the answers I want. Sure it's true. The economy does do all those things. Isn't it the case that the particular kind of economy we have has a tremendous and profound effect on all sides of life? The economy influences culture, and government, and kinship—of course it does. It's the notion that the economy alone has defining influences that is problematic.

And what if we ask the same thing about other orientations? What if an anarchist says the polity is the base and the rest is the superstructure? Can she make similar claims to those that the Marxist makes for the economy, but now about the polity impacting all sides of life? And what about the feminist or nationalist? Can only one or two legitimately make claims about their priority domain of life impacting others, or can they all reasonably make such claims?

This is the kind of question we have to ask to move on. For example, how do family structure and kinship structure impact the economy or the state or the culture? What are the most profound and influential ways the kinship sphere influences what goes on in the economy? It's not easy to answer. The people who have done it really well, I think, have made real contributions.

So what's different about what we're doing than what others have already done?

Well we're not putting one of the spheres at the bottom and everything else on top of that. We're putting people at the bottom and all four spheres in some kind of entwined and interactive combination around them setting up an institutional boundary that people relate to. And we then have to figure out how the people and institutions interact with each other. How we define a society and how we characterize it will be based on what those relationships are. How we distinguish societies will be based on that. How historical change happens will derive from that. What a revolution is for us and what social evolution is for us will also arise from this understanding we have of society and its aspects. These are some of the subjects of coming chapters. Then later we'll also get into goals and once we have in mind some worthy goals, into how we develop a revolutionary strategy to attain them. What does it mean to talk about a revolutionary strategy? Who are the agents? How do they function? What are the components of revolutionary strategy? What does the theory tell us about such things, and so on? That's where we are headed.

Before we go on—what about socialism? What is socialism, in this developing framework?

It is a vision that is typically associated with Marxism, which we have said a bit about already, and will say more about as we continue.

What about democratic socialism?

If you mean as a school of thought, it too is a variant of Marxism. Has anybody heard of any other combination theories?

Anarcho-feminism?

Yes, anarcho-feminism, sure.

Marxist-feminism?

Yes.

Eco-anarchism?

Yes, and what is going on here? Marxist-nationalism. Socialist-feminism. What are these things? What's going on?

What's going on is that instead of looking at society through one sphere, all of a sudden there is a major breakthrough, and we look at society through two spheres, or by way of a context and a sphere. It might be that what we're saying is that we'll look at society through two spheres that are separate but both influential, as with Marxist-feminism. In that case, we use the concepts from one framework or the concepts from the other, whichever is appropriate to our situation at the moment. But then in addition women came up with another label, socialist-feminism, to designate a way of looking at society and history from two spheres that interactively affect one another. If we are socialist-feminists we use adapted concepts from each of the two frameworks at once. All the different obscure leftist frameworks are just different ways of coming at society that each yield a somewhat different tool box of concepts (or combination of tool boxes or reformed tool boxes) which we use, and as a result see history somewhat differently. And there is virtually every permutation and combination of these things in existence that you can think of, with some of them more popular than are others.

And so the obvious point is that I have a permutation/combination that I favor too, and that we are together working on. Mine is to take all four spheres, and therefore all four orientations, and to adapt each in light of the impact of the others— except for one thing. I'll give away a bit now, before we get to the later stages, in part because the real process of developing theory isn't as linear and step-by-step logical as the way people write about theories after the fact. There are jumps and leaps. There are intuitions in the early stages that bear on later stages. It isn't just discovering step-by-step, but sometimes we are seeking toward something already pre-envisioned. But please, understand that I don't want to discuss at length yet what I will now foreshadow. I just want to reveal that yes, ideas like the following were in mind as this intellectual framework was first being built, even in part guiding the process.

So, back when these ideas were first emerging, I felt already that for a good theory we would need a theory of each sphere. So a theory of polity would be anarchism maybe. And a theory of the gender sphere would be feminism maybe. And a theory of the cultural sphere would be nationalism maybe. And a theory of the economic sphere would be Marxism maybe. I in fact thought, from my experience in movements back in the Sixties, that nationalism, anarchism, and feminism were plausible places to start for those spheres because they represented the expression of the needs and interests of the oppressed sectors of people in each of those spheres as those folks tried to formulate their experiences and interests into an understanding of how their focused sphere works. Those partial frameworks needed refinement, I thought, mostly in light of accounting for the considerable (and at that time very much underestimated) impact of the other three spheres on the one focused sphere of each framework— but still they were potentially good starting points for each sphere.

But regarding the economy, I thought Marxism failed to meet even that criterion. It would take us too far afield to explore this closely, but I came to the conclusion quite early that Marxism doesn't represent the interests of working people developed into a conception of the economy. That doesn't mean that Marxism is all wrong. There are all sorts of things about Marxism that are right. Just like there are various things about bourgeois economic theory, for that matter that are right, though that isn't the theory that I want to use either.

At any rate, for the economy, I thought we'd need to more or less start over. And that made me cautious about everything, and propelled me to think about concepts from scratch. What it was about Marxism that deterred me from thinking it was a plausible place to look for economic concepts isn't all that important just yet, but suffice it to say, that in addition to being narrow (a problem with all the frameworks), Marxism was wrong at its roots about economics itself. Marxism understood the importance of private property in the emergence of opposed classes, but it misunderstood, in fact it largely ignored and even obscured the importance of differential conditions of work in class definitions, and this failing undercut the value of many parts of its analysis, and even more drastically, of its agenda.

4. Accommodation and Co-Definition

> Concepts which have proved useful for ordering things easily assume so great an authority over us, that we forget their terrestrial origin and accept them as unalterable facts. They then become labeled as 'conceptual necessities,' etc. The road of scientific progress is frequently blocked for long periods by such errors. It is therefore not just an idle game to exercise our ability to analyze familiar concepts, and to demonstrate the conditions on which this justification of their usefulness depends.
>
> –Albert Einstein

We have society. We have four spheres of social activity. We understand that an institution might be in more than one sphere, and that actually most institutions are, at least in some sense, in all four. An institution will accomplish some of the function of each of the four spheres, but might predominantly fit one of them.

What would a school be? A school is a workplace, but it is also certainly a cultural institution. A school is a community institution, but it's a governing institution. What is it mostly?

An economic institution?

It's an economic institution because it has inputs and outputs and partakes in fulfilling an economic function of society, yes. But I would say it's mostly a kinship institution because its main focus is socialization. The way we've defined our concepts, that seems sensible to me. But if someone else defines their concepts differently, the whole discussion will take a different turn. But that's the way we've defined them, so that's the way the discussion goes for us. That's what a theory does for us: it organizes how we ask questions, how we look at things, how we make connections. If it does this well, it directs us to not only true features, but also to features important to what we care about influencing.

To understand a society, people take different approaches. Some people put a single aspect in a fundamental position and say that that aspect is at the heart of the society—the fulcrum around which all else revolves. Once we understand that aspect and its interrelations, they suggest, we pretty much understand the whole society because that aspect emanates influences that contour everything else, and changing that aspect can change the whole.

For example, what's the aspect that emanates influence to contour everything else for a Marxist?

The economy.

Yes, the Marxist is basically saying that there among all the features in society the economy's special character is its defining influence. Akin to a force field, the influence emanates from the economy and pushes into every other feature in society to mold and contour and even define them.

Well, is there any truth to that? Does the economy have these defining influences that emanate out and affect things?

Yeah. I think it does.

Sure it does. But is this a full enough approach to understanding society? Well, sure it is if utilizing it orients us sufficiently to understand what's going on in society and history so as to proceed as we need to. But what does a feminist say, in contrast to the Marxist viewpoint? And what does an anarchist say? What do they put—

The state.

Yes, the anarchist looks at the same world and sees the state and polity emanating a force field that influences everything else. And the feminist sees the kinship sphere and the family doing it. And the nationalist sees identity and culture doing it.

Okay. And they can all make compelling arguments that what they highlight impacts all the rest.

Suppose we return to our approach. We've got four spheres of social life with their institutions and their role structures and they each, at least in our society, generate a hierarchy of constituencies. So they generate class structure; racial structure and racial hierarchies and cultural identity hierarchies; gender hierarchies; and political hierarchies.

We can next ask how these spheres relate to one another.

To begin toward an answer, suppose that in the kinship sphere of a particular society there is patriarchy and so men have a dominant position with respect to women. What might be the case regarding gender in the same society's economy?

We know that one possibility is that there too men are in a dominant position with respect to women. But what's another possibility? Perhaps women are in the dominant position, or men and women are in comparable positions. So, you could at least imagine a case in which within a society you have a kinship sphere that is patriarchal and continually reproducing the conditions of men dominating women, but over in the same society's economy men and women are dispersed throughout roles randomly. Maybe there are even instances in which women are occupying better roles. If women were occupying better roles in the economy and the kinship sphere was patriarchal, what would be the state of the society?

It wouldn't function. It would be a mess.

Why do you say that? What do you mean?

The women would use their knowledge and power gained in the economy to subvert the men at home and take over.

Yes, or vice versa. The men, having gotten a dominant position in kinship would try to reverse their subordination in the economy. Sure you could imagine this, unless you're a Marxist, in which case you think the economic sphere's relationship inevitably defines the rest, such that patriarchy would inevitably unravel in the face of economic equity. For the careful Marxist the hierarchy in families, socialization, procreation, and sexuality is incapable of redefining the economy and imposing a gender division there. But in fact it is possible, isn't it? In fact, it is what we have seen historically.

In any case, whatever you believe about that, the conceptual issue of how we understand the four spheres goes a step further to address the influences and effects of each sphere on the nature of the others.

Well, as we have already intimated we can certainly see the possibility of accommodation of imposed hierarchies. Accommodation between spheres means that the pecking order established by each sphere comes into a non-disruptive correspondence with what is happening in the others.

How does that happen?

Well, the idea that the Marxist had, and the feminist had, and the others had, of one sphere emanating influences that affect the others rings true. So the kinship sphere emanates an influence of men above women, which involves various suppositions and biases and beliefs and patterns of activity and resources. And this emanation, which we call sexism, and which arises in the kinship sphere, spreads over into the economy despite the fact that economic logic per se doesn't have anything in it that would place men above women. There's nothing about economic logic that leads to that. It doesn't derive from purely economic influences. But the pressure arising from kinship could cause there to be a pay scale that rewards men more than women, for example, so that the hierarchy in the economy doesn't conflict with that which is central to kinship relations.

But could anything even more substantial happen? If there is patriarchy, could something happen to the economy as a result of it, more than simply accommodating to sexism, that is?

This is one of the harder questions we will encounter, I think. The first thing that could happen, which is clear enough and which people already have a feeling for, is that insofar as there are good jobs and bad jobs, we might be distributing them in the economy to accommodate to the hierarchy born in the kinship sphere. And insofar as there is high pay and low pay, these too might be distributed in the economy to create the same hierarchical order that arises in the kinship sphere. And the reason this process occurs is so the two don't clash, or, put differently, it is the condition reached when the clashes come more or less to their conclusion. So we see that the views and expectations that people have regarding their relative position in a male/female ordering, as created in each sphere, accommodate. If they don't accommodate, conditions in the two spheres are at odds, and one or both are likely to change due to pressure from the other until there is sufficient accommodation to reduce those pressures. So that is one possible outcome, for sure. But there's an even more profound possibility.

All the wealth goes to the males?

That's the same possibility, accommodation, made extreme. However the fact that the allocation of wealth in an economy respects the expectations of male dominance over women born in a sexist kinship sphere doesn't necessitate, in most societies, such an extreme result. And economic logic itself doesn't require gender hierarchy, unless it exists for other reasons. Economic logic can ignore gender difference, just as it can ignore differences in height, weight, hair color, etc., if there is no other logic aggravating economics into incorporating oppressive gradations between men and women. But if we put patriarchal kinship into the society along with economy, then for economy to accord with neighboring kinship, women and men will be pressured to distribute among economic roles unequally. By pure economic logic they would be randomly distributed, but now they're distributed in a hierarchy, or, if not, there is pressure in the opposite direction, against patriarchy in kinship. That's what we understand so far. But there's another possibility. Suppose something more happens. Suppose the economic roles themselves change. The forces emanating from kinship cause the economic institutions themselves to change in their very definition and logic.

Each theoretical school is going to be able to easily understand this in only one direction. The Marxist understands the idea of the economy emanating influences that affect the very definition and nature of the other spheres—not just causing them to respect class hierarchies, merely accommodating, but literally altering their defining features. The Marxist has no trouble anticipating this, seeing it, predicting it, and thinking about how it impacts his or her agendas due to their belief in the ability of the economy to redefine family or culture or state. The feminist, nationalist, and anarchist understand the same dynamic, but in each case with the influencing sphere that redefines the basic features of the others reflecting their respective priority: kinship, community/cultural, and polity. Due to the influence of their concepts on their perceptions, as well as their personal experience and identities, few of these folks, particularly in trying circumstances, perceive that their own focused sphere could be similarly redefined by influences from without.

Let's look at this more closely. Suppose you are a Marxist. We have a society and we know its economy is capitalist. It has a kinship sphere and its logic of procreation and socialization leads to certain sexist roles in households. When we drop that kinship sphere alongside the capitalist economy, what could happen to the two?

"Well," the Marxist answers, "the families will become arrayed in a class hierarchy. The distribution of wealth that they have will comply with class orderings." But another Marxist might suggest it's much more than that; that is, the kinship institutions themselves, the actual roles, might be affected by class pressures. Families' behavior will come to depend on which class they are in, on the way the economy impacts the roles of parenting and socializing, on how the economy changes their logic. So you begin to have not merely mothers and fathers, but bourgeois or working-class mothers and fathers, and these become quite different. Marxists understand this possibility, at least in principle. Families might have different role structures and patterns, in important and defining ways, depending on their class position. And this is worth investigating because it is true that the economy often does emanate influences that go right into the role structures of the kinship sphere to affect their very definitions, not just causing them to accommodate the incomes of families, but affecting their internal role structures. In fact, for the good Marxist this is a central part of understanding society: How does the economic sphere impact other aspects of life, not only causing an accommodation that respects class hierarchy, but also literally redefining various aspects of key institutions elsewhere in society according to economic logic? Well, okay, that's fine as far as it goes, but in contrast what does the feminist understand?

The same thing, but now it's gender that is defining the economy and everything else?

Precisely so. That is what she sees as compared to the Marxist. The expectations built into the foundational concepts in their different conceptual tool boxes point them at reality differently. Of course one of them might be right and one wrong—or both could be partly right and partly wrong. We have to look at actual phenomena to judge that.

Our feminist pays attention to the same kind of dynamic between these two spheres of social life, for example, as the Marxist, but in reverse. When a woman named Batya Weinbaum looked at the economy—she's a very strong feminist—she saw mothers and fathers in the workplace. She didn't see only bosses and workers. She saw mothers and fathers and even aunts and uncles. She saw behavior and structure emanating from nuclear families pushing into the economy. In other words, she saw a replication of kinship relations inside the economy. So this feminist was saying, "Look, the kinship sphere is so powerful it can redefine how people carry out economic activity." Similarly the Marxist says that the economic sphere is so powerful it can redefine how people procreate and socialize, and the nationalist deems the cultural sphere so powerful as to redefine both families and economy, and the anarchist says that the political sphere is so powerful—well, what does the anarchist say?

They say that hierarchy comes from the political and affects every-thing else.

Exactly. The kinship sphere as seen by Batya Weinbaum not only pulls the economy into accommodation with what is happening in kin relations—making women rank below men in the economic hierarchy as they do in the kinship hierarchy—but also redefines economic roles by affecting the very logic of economic activity. Roles in the economy aimed at accomplishing production, consumption, and allocation begin to incorporate logic and structure deriving from the kinship sphere such that activity in the economy is, after this effect takes hold, not only reproducing class, but also reproducing sexism as well.

The key conceptual point is that this relationship is possible. In some society, it might not happen. In some other society, it might happen. We might look at a society and see that this high level of influence from one sphere to some other is not there. But we can conceive of how it could be there, and could be profoundly important. And that means we have to look to see if it is there. And that means we require concepts that propel us to look for this influence rather than blind us to its possibility.

So first, we can conceive of any of the four spheres we've high-lighted accommodating one another. That means one sphere coming into accommodation sufficiently so as not to disrupt the defining hierarchy established by other spheres. In other words, the dynamics in the economy, for example, bend regarding treatment of women as compared to men, or regarding Blacks as compared to Whites, until they don't disrupt the hierarchy that emerges in other spheres. But beyond this accommodation, we can also imagine that the economy actually starts to change so that the job roles in the economy, for example, begin to embody sexist characteristics that originate in kinship relations. It isn't just that good and bad jobs are divided among men and women to respect the ordering that kinship established. Rather, the role of secretary vis-à-vis employer begins to take on certain gender characteristics reproducing certain relationships beyond the intrinsic economic logic of accomplishing tasks in tune with class norms, or even in tune with class norms and accommodat-ing pecking orders emerging elsewhere. As a result, the tasks are di-vided up in such a way that there are sexist roles in the economy that wouldn't have been there solely by economic logic. And of course this isn't only about jobs, but also allocation, consumption, and so on.

Just like a nurse...

Yes, the particular things that a nurse does in our economy, aren't, I think, a function only of economic logic, but owe their character also to the impact of the gender sphere. And you can imagine a change in what nurses do, indeed, in tune with changes in the relation of women to kinship. So Weinbaum, unlike those using a different conceptual tool box, could see these kinds of impacts throughout the economy. She could see sexist role definitions that can't have their origin solely in economic logic and she could see them not just in the obvious places such as families, but in General Motors and in the dynamics of economic exchange. So, that's very interesting and powerful.

To see the power of it, and getting a bit ahead of ourselves, what's an implication of seeing society as a meshing of these four spheres of social life for a strategy that radicals might develop?

You might focus on trying to change the sphere that affects you most. Or even the one that you think is the foundation of how all society is.

Yes, that is a perfectly sensible first reaction to the picture of a society that has four spheres. You of course want to be efficient, so you want to focus your energies on the part of society that you think is emanating the key influences affecting everything, and which, if altered, could alter everything. Later on, having altered those most basic and generally influential aspects, you can fiddle around at the edges and change some lower order stuff that hasn't altered already. And we can also see why somebody else reacting to this type analysis might get frustrated.

Suppose, for example, I'm a Marxist and you're a feminist. And I say, "Let's do class struggle," and you tell me to forget it. And I say to you, "No, I'm not saying your feminist concerns don't matter, I'm not saying gender doesn't matter. I'm saying, precisely because you rightly want to get rid of gender oppression, come join me and advance the class struggle, because that's the easiest way to do it."

And you tell me that feminism matters—and you mean not only that you care about feminism, but that it is at society's foundation. And now we're talking past each other. Because I may think that feminism really matters. I could think that women's plight was abysmal, for example, but strategically I could nonetheless also think that the right way to address women's oppression is to go after the economy via class struggle. And in turn you might think that of course economics is important. But the way to go after economic justice is to address the family and sex and gender roles first. Changes made in the primary sphere, kinship, will percolate through and redefine everything else. And once that's done we can move on to address secondary tasks left to do elsewhere.

Conflicts between radical schools of thought often seem to be about differences in what they deem most hurtful and therefore most urgent, but they are usually really about what is deemed more influential and therefore more strategic. So what they're really arguing about is something conceptual, something theoretical, and something strategic, though it usually devolves into an argument about what hurts more—about what's moral and what isn't—which is, in fact, not the issue. What hurts and what doesn't aren't the issue. Everyone can agree on how much oppressions hurt, yet still profoundly disagree on what to do about them. Finding which factors emanate defining influences that reproduce hurtful conditions is the issue.

Sensible disagreements between radical schools of thought are about causes and effects. If you're the radical feminist and I tell you that I want to change the workplace, you could reply, "Well sure, I do too, so come help me change the family, come help me change socialization. These are the best way to change the workplace most effectively." And I maintain that I think the workplace is important. And you say back to me, "Look, I agree that the workplace is important. But now you need to get serious about it. Come help me change the family. Come help me change the stuff that, if it changes, will change your workplace." And you get frustrated. Or vice versa.

And now here is an interesting, rarely noticed, ironic point about these disputes. The more one side is right, if it's in favor of one of the single-focus perspectives, the more that side is also wrong. That is, suppose you are a strong feminist so you feel that the feminist sphere emanates a very powerful influence throughout society, redefining relations in other spheres and not just in its own. Okay, if you are right, what does that mean?

That gender impacts everything else very much.

Yes, and what does that tell us likely happens to the other spheres? How will they have been influenced? It isn't just that they'll line up with kinship, right? It isn't just that they will accommodate to the gender hierarchy born in kinship relations?

No, if the feminist's stronger claim is right then the other spheres will be molded by gender: their roles will be redefined.

Yes, exactly so. That is what the radical feminist is saying. She is arguing that the economy and culture and all facets of society will be bent by forces emanating from the kinship sphere so they'll embody a kinship-originated logic and in turn reproduce kinship hierarchies, norms, and roles by their own actions. So what happens now? If I, the radical feminist, am really right about how important kinship is, then the economy will become a site of the reproduction of patriarchy. The more I'm right about how important the kinship sphere is, the more it's the case that the economy and the polity and the culture are going to reproduce kinship relations that I despise. So even if I only want to change kinship, what's my problem?

Because kinship is so powerful all the other spheres are creating sexism too?

Yes. That is the irony. Suppose I am a radical feminist and I do my feminist revolution and I change just the kinship sphere. Have I even dealt with patriarchy?

Not fully, because there are going to be powerful influences from the other spheres back toward the old kinship relations.

Exactly, because the old kinship mode was so damn powerful. I got rid of some of the current roots of kinship, to be sure, but before I did so they had spread their logic all over the rest of society. They'd taken up residence in the other spheres. So I haven't even gotten rid of all the roots reproducing sexism, only a part of them. The irony is that the stronger the radical feminist's claims are that the kinship sphere emanates defining influences throughout society, the more true it is that the radical feminist's strategy needs to address society's other spheres as well—even if she cares only about gender hierarchy.

And notice that the same thing holds for the Marxist. If the Marxist is right that class forces are so powerful that they have profound influence throughout society, then they will likely turn the family into a site for creating class consciousness. And they will do that throughout the society, including in the culture and in the state. So if Marxists just change the economy, the notion that they've thereby changed the whole class-creating dynamic of society will be wrong. By their own logic they will have changed the economy and though they may hope that everything else will change in turn, at least regarding class relations, in fact it's also possible and even probable that instead they'll have reached the type of unstable situation we talked about earlier. They will have attained a new economy, with fledgling class norms, yes. But the society will have old highly established culture and kinship and state, and these will have been so powerfully impacted by the old economy that the Marxists uprooted that they aren't just passive about old economic forms, but actively try to re-impose them. So now the Marxists have a changed economy, but all the other spheres are trying to reproduce the old economy. The non-economic spheres of society are reproducing people with expectations and capacities suited to the old economy. So the people emerging from other spheres don't fit the new economy, and the people emerging from the new economy don't fit the society's other spheres. Pressures arise for continuing change, but it may not go the way the Marxist hopes it will, especially if he is paying little or ill-informed attention to the nature of society's other spheres. So even if the Marxist cares only about class relations, the more adamant the Marxist is about the power of the economic sphere's impact on other institutions throughout society, the more of a priority it ought to be for him to address those other institutions too.

> *But if you change the focused sphere—the key structure, the main variable—then wouldn't the advocate of that approach argue that the other spheres would fall in line eventually?*

Yes, they certainly tend to argue that, though I think it is inconsistent of them to do so because by their own claims it also may not happen. In any event, they should want to make it most probable, and that requires the larger conceptual and strategic orientation. Of course, for us things are different. Given our framework, we won't make a claim like theirs in the first place. For us to move beyond discussing what is conceivable to identifying what is actually present in some society, we have to look at the specific society itself. But to create a framework for looking at it in a way that doesn't preclude seeing some real and important possibility, we have to develop concepts that focus us on what is possible or likely and that also don't prevent us from seeing anything that is important.

To go on, and hopefully things will become clearer at every level of the meaning of all this as we develop it further, we said earlier one possibility is that a society could be in a condition where these spheres are really out of whack. (That's a technical term in our framework by the way, "out of whack," which when pronounced properly is one word, outawack, of course.) So, consider the United States' economy and cultural sphere during and right after World War II. Was there any outawackness then?

Yes. Women in the workplace.

That's one sort of outawackness, yes, or, in our more formal terms, of non-accommodation, but there was another as well. Yours is an example of gender and the economy. There's another one similar to that. What was going on in the army?

Integration?

Yes, in the army, relatively speaking, Whites and Blacks and others were working together, trusting one another, getting past prejudices, etc. And at this time, racism in the U.S. was so extreme that to be in proximity and functioning together was a real leap from the familiar into something quite subversive. So we had social spheres outawack. While racial and sexual hierarchies weren't entirely undone by integration in the army or by the entry of women into men's slots in the economy while men were off at war, still the integrated army and the entry of women in the workforce were considerably outawack with the rest of the culture and gender relations of society. And over time during the war that was a very powerful cause of lots of changes including the emergence of the women's movement and especially the civil rights movement. If you look closely, that is, and you ask where the roots of these were, you find them in these new relations in different parts of society—the military and the wartime economy—that got outawack and raised conflicting expectations generating conflicting mindsets and behaviors. Different spheres of society can move from accommodating to not accommodating. But the more likely condition, on average, is that society rolls along with different spheres accommodating to one another pretty closely, or perhaps even wholly reproducing one another.

Okay, so we can have accommodation and now we see that we can have what we might call co-definition, as well. That's as good a label as any for the process of spheres actually redefining one another's basic relations: co-definition. And then we also have the germ of an idea that if spheres co-define strongly enough they may get to be co-reproducing, so perhaps that could be another useful concept.

What do you think of all this? Are we just running in circles, or are we adding useful concepts to our conceptual tool box? Does what we're doing seem in tune with your prior views? Does it challenge them? Does it broaden or alter them? Does it make them more precise or easier to enunciate? These are things to think and talk about in preparation for next chapter.

5. Social Evolution and Revolution

The legitimate purpose of abstraction in social science is never to get away from the real world but rather to isolate certain aspects of the real world for intensive investigation. When, therefore, we say that we are operating at a high level of abstraction, we mean that we are dealing with a relatively small number of aspects of reality; we emphatically do not mean that those aspects with which we are dealing are not capable of historical investigation and factual illustration.

–Paul Sweezy

Suppose we look at a particular society and we ask how should we identify it. How should we categorize a society?

By the character of its institutions?

Which institutions?

I would say kinship.

Why?

Because whether a society follows the female or male line will make differences in everything, especially in their economics and probably everything else as well.

I asked the question, and you answered it from your prior expectations and inclinations. But you didn't answer it in the context of the framework we are developing. That's fine, of course, if it is your considered view. But, since we are experimenting with developing a new perspective, in that context, your answer is not so good. And I think this is a very important thing to learn. To develop a way of looking at things, we have to respect our experience and intuitions, of course, but we also have to give our conceptual creations a chance. We have to use them, and if they fail, fine, then fix them or fall back on prior beliefs. But if we can make them work, and if they lead us to new insights, well, that's good. We just finished implying last chapter that it's very likely that all four social spheres affect changes in one another and in the whole society.

Well everything does that, but gender factors seem to be so strong—

Gender factors are strong. That's true. But what if someone else says that those capitalist class factors seem to be so strong, or that dictatorial state deems to be so strong, or that apartheid culture seems to be so strong? Aren't those claims correct as well?

The Marxist believes that economic factors are always strongest, always dominant from the point of view of what you need to address to win lasting change. The feminist believes the same thing, but of gender factors. The nationalist believes it for culture. The anarchist believes it for power and the state. But in our framework, we don't believe any of this ahead of time. In a particular society, our approach says maybe one sphere is more dominant than others, or maybe not.

Well, it's what you notice when you examine society, isn't it?

I don't want to give a wrong impression. Society is what it is. If you don't notice that it has families, it doesn't mean it doesn't have families. If one sphere is dominant and you deny it, that doesn't mean it isn't dominant. Likewise, if four spheres are co-reproducing but when you look at it you see only the economy having outward effects and feel the other three are quite secondary or even peripheral, just because that's what you see and that's what your concepts allow you to perceive, doesn't make you correct. It is what you see, but it isn't what's there.

So yes, society is what you notice, if you notice what's there—which is to say if you are very perceptive, very open to the reality that you encounter in all its facets, and if you are not bending what you see to fit whatever preconceptions you may hold. And as we've begun to understand, your perceptivity is going to depend partly on where you look, partly on how you organize and relate to what you see, and then of course also partly on the effort and care that you employ. Concepts set the stage. The ideas in your head organize your thoughts, direct your eyes and mind, and help determine the degree to which what you see is what's there.

So you personally might happen to see gender having a priority impact. Yes, but we don't want to have a theory which names each society as a particular type based on what some specific people primarily notice because of their particular backgrounds. We want an approach that's broad and objective, and also suited to our social change project. We want an approach that goes beyond what I or you happen to be sensitized to. Indeed, that's what theory is about. If a quick look around reveals everything important, why bother to develop a special conceptual tool box to help us hone in on what is truly important?

Let's consider the other theories we have discussed so far, for a moment. What do they do? Well, like any theory, they orient a person and contour what a person sees. The Marxist, feminist, anarchist and nationalist offer different answers to the questions of what's important in society, how to name it, and how to examine it. One or another of these approaches may be more often true, and may be chosen for only that good reason. But it is also possible that these theories are chosen because they replicate the sensitization of the person utilizing them, and that they in turn further sensitize the person to dynamics they already most easily perceive, but desensitize the person to dynamics they don't easily perceive or even generally misperceive.

In other words, the person who becomes a feminist, a Marxist, a nationalist, or an anarchist may have been highly attuned to the importance of the sphere featured by their chosen theory even before adopting the theory, due to their life experiences. And the adopted conceptual framework may have then ratified their prior prioritization and made it even stronger. And the person may well have been weak at discerning the dynamics of other spheres of social life, or even apt to misperceive them before choosing the theory; and then the chosen theory not only didn't counter this tendency, but also perhaps aggravated it.

Because all four spheres are generally very important, someone lean-ing toward seeing one as always more important needs to be pushed in a new direction?

Yes, exactly. You don't want a person's conceptual tool box to aggravate the person's experiential tendency to only see one sphere as important, at least if more than one can be important. You want the chosen concepts to counter that typical bias and to open up the person to seeing more. We can actually explore this issue further by returning to the problem of naming societies by type.

The Marxist calls societies capitalist or feudal or socialist. The feminist might call them matriarchal or patriarchal. A nationalist might label one society apartheid or label another society white supremacist. And in doing so, each of these theorists might feel that they've captured the essence of the whole society by naming the one sphere and calling the whole society after that one sphere's features. The other alternative is to use some list of names taking account of all four spheres or maybe even to come up with a word that captures all four.

But let's continue with our hypothetical society. In this society, what is a revolution? First of all, it's whatever we say it is. That is, revolution is a new concept that we're defining, so we can have it point to whatever we like, as long as what it points to corresponds, of course, to real conditions. We want this new concept, revolution, to have use for us, which means we want it to divide off some aspect of reality that we want to pay special attention to. But nobody is over-seeing us here. We don't have to settle for the dictionary definition, or for some famous person's definition. We want to develop a concept useful for us. So what definition should we use? How should we define the concept revolution so it will be useful for us? What aspect of reality should we have the word revolution point to so that the word names something we care to pay special attention to?

A fundamental change in one of the spheres.

Okay, one way we can define it is a fundamental change in one of the spheres. Or we might define it as a fundamental change in all four of the spheres. Or we might say only a fundamental change in the economic sphere is a revolution—the rest is something else. Or only a fundamental change in kinship is a revolution, and the rest is something else. Or we might say a fundamental change in any of them is a revolution.

So now we have two problems. We have to choose which of these possibilities to settle on, and what the word fundamental means. We don't want revolution to refer merely to any change, obviously, because then you would have a revolution every thirty seconds. It must be a fundamental change, something far less frequent. So what's that?

Fundamental meaning that maybe it changes the role structure within the boundary.

Now we are getting the hang of this theory-building project. We are trying to develop new concepts, yes, but within the broad rubric of what we already have. Excellent. Fundamental means that it changes the role structure. How?

It changes the institutions in some basic way.

It changes the institutions, and since the institutions are just a sum total of the role structures, it must be a change in the role structures. But an evolutionary change alters the role structures, doesn't it? Suppose you are at work and the job definitions are jumbled, made different from before. It's a change in the roles, certainly. But it isn't likely to be what we mean by a revolution, is it? That is, do we want to have the concept revolution refer to that, or don't we? Let's jump back a step from revolution to evolution and see if we can get at what we are trying to designate that way. What's an evolutionary change in a society?

Gradual?

But what makes it evolutionary?

It's inevitable?

Well, no, I don't think so. First, there is nothing inevitable about most changes that happen in society. Take the shifting of jobs mentioned earlier, or some new invention, or a corporation moving overseas, or birth control being discovered and made available at some moment, and so on. None of these changes have to happen when they do, or how they do, or even at all. Second, events that are inevitable are in fact not very important for us to analyze, precisely because we can't do anything much about them. They are not going to have a very paramount place in our conceptual framework for just that reason. For example, death is absolutely inevitable but that's exactly why we don't have a movement against it and why it isn't going to play a big role in our conceptual tool box. Yes, death is important. But it's not just importance that makes phenomena critical to us. Death's annoying, to say the least, and it's important and it isn't fun and it's painful, but should we organize against it? Not when it's inevitable. And in fact—and this is something we will return to again much later—that's why some people don't organize for what we organize for. Because they think it's just as stupid to do what we do as we think it is to stand on the corner and argue against death. In other words, death is inevitable in our view, so we don't oppose it with our activism—what a silly waste of time that would be. Oppression is inevitable for them, so they don't oppose it with their activism. It's the same idea. It's just that one's wrong and one's right. Okay, so where were we.

What's an evolutionary change?

One of the features that you said characterized a revolution was a change in the role structures. Suppose we see the emergence of computer programmer as a new role. Is that an evolutionary change or a revolutionary change? In other words, we have a society, it's coasting along and we see the emergence of a new role: computer programmer.

It's an evolutionary change.

Sure, we know that it's evolutionary even if we don't yet know precisely why.

It comes from the existing structure.

I think you may be getting closer to clarifying what we intuitively identify, but everything's going to come from the past unless it comes from Mars. So it all comes from the past, and that can't be the distinguishing factor. What's more important is that it's consistent with the past, which is perhaps what you meant. It does what?

It reinforces the past.

Yes. It continues the basic defining features of what was there before.

It's an outgrowth of the past, sure, but everything's going to be an outgrowth of the past. If it's not an outgrowth of the past, where did it come from? But more to the point, it is consistent with the past. It continues to reproduce the defining features of the past, as they have been. It doesn't change the defining features of the past. But now we have the problem of figuring out what the defining features are—another concept. That's theory building: creating one new concept after another. You ask a question that seems important to you. You try to answer with your already developed conceptual framework. If you can do that, that's great. If you can't do it, then you develop new concepts by finding new features to highlight and work with until you can answer your question. Then new questions arise, and so on.

Suppose that there is apartheid in South Africa and then there's not apartheid in South Africa. Is that a revolution?

Because it's sudden?

No, I don't care how long this change takes, and in fact it was actually a long struggle with many stages. We have apartheid, and then we don't, and I want to know whether that change is a revolution or not. Do we want to define the word revolution so that this is a revolution, or so that it isn't? Anybody want to say it isn't a revolution?

Yeah.

Why?

It depends on how it's going to be achieved.

Well, if we define the concept that way, then by definition you will be right that the designation does depend on how change is achieved. But is that the most fruitful way to define the concept? Is that what we want to highlight? We could say a revolution is a change that comes about after someone gets shot, or after there is some level of violence, or in some short time period, or on Sundays, if we wanted to. But why do this? Is this honing us in on what we really want to be highlighting with this concept? On what we want this label to be pointing to?

Suppose we define revolution as a change in the defining characteristics of a sphere of social life that is brought about by *x*, and then we fill in the blank by saying what x is. X may be violence, or tumultuous upheaval, or government edict, or whatever. We can put any one of those variables in and then revolutions would be determined by how the events came about. But do we really want to put such a criterion in there? Does it matter how it was brought about? Is that the key feature?

Some people will want to define revolution as being brought about by violence, or whatever. I don't want to define it that way, however. You might be right that it's a better way to define it; it might be useful to have a concept that focuses us on how events came about. And then you would develop that concept and maybe many others differently than I would. And using the concepts, you would see the tapestry that is a society and history perhaps a bit differently than I would, organize your data differently, and find distinct connections. And you might, as a result, perceive things that I missed or you might miss things that I perceived. And these differences might matter in thinking about our agendas, and we might even weigh these differences when choosing between our two approaches, even if they both corresponded to reality, as far as they went.

So, returning to the question, it seems to me that transcending apartheid is a revolution because—

It changed the fundamental characteristics of the community sphere.

Yes. However it happened. Even if it happened by mistake.

And in turn it changed all four areas. Every sphere is changed.

Now why is that? Why if apartheid changes, is every sphere going to change? Or, if they don't, if every sphere doesn't change, what's going on?

Well, apartheid, when it existed, emanated influences all over society. Some of those influences just caused other spheres to accommodate with the cultural hierarchies of apartheid. Blacks earned way less than Whites, occupied lesser jobs, etc. Some of those influences may have caused other spheres to co-reproduce apartheid. Perhaps the economy was itself reproducing apartheid in the actual divisions of labor and job definitions. Families were themselves reproducing apartheid in the patterns of socialization. The state was reproducing apartheid in the definition of its roles and laws, and so on. We'd have to look to see. It could have been that way, or it might not have been that way. We don't know without looking.

Now, suppose you get rid of apartheid in the cultural/community sphere. You must also get rid of the political state that was creating apartheid or change it, and you get rid of or change the economy that was producing apartheid, and you get rid of or change the socialization and kinship patterns that were reproducing apartheid; otherwise you've got apartheid being reproduced by those other spheres and apartheid being un-produced, so to speak, by the new community sphere, and your society ends up unstable. Perhaps that is what South Africa may be enduring right now, by the way. They did get rid of apartheid in the community sphere, for the most part, and they are, in fact, winning the battle, I think, of changing the other spheres, at least regarding apartheid, but certainly not fully yet, and things could still revert. So let's say, whatever we might truly find after a serious examination, that apartheid is mostly gone from one sphere and on the way out across society. Would that mean the other spheres are fully liberated?

No.

Because?

The change is fundamental in one sphere and not in the others so the other conditions still exist and are rooted elsewhere.

Yes. And the oppressive features that originate in other spheres and haven't been eliminated are going to impose limits on how much of a gain for humanity the change away from apartheid is. This is pretty straightforward and simple, but when we organize it conceptually by having tools that highlight it and attune us to it, it becomes even simpler and clearer. And it eliminates a whole lot of hassle that arises from talking vaguely about these matters.

So suppose we define revolution as a fundamental transformation in the defining relations in at least one of the four social spheres. Then we could look at history and ask if the events in the Soviet Union in 1917 were revolutionary. Now if so, in which sphere?

Yes, in the economic and political spheres.

Yes, we believe there was a revolution in the economic sphere because there used to be a hierarchy of capitalist/coordinator/worker and it was done away with and became one of just coordinator/worker. That is, there used to be some folks who owned the means of production; and below them some who had a relative monopoly on economic decision-making positions, skills, and conceptual labor as managers and other conceptual empowered agents; and below them the more traditional workers. But then, after the change, the capitalists were gone—no longer the ruling class, no longer present at all, in fact. That's different. And the defining economic institutions that used to be private ownership and the market for allocation became instead public ownership or state ownership and central planning for allocation. That's different. So the basic core defining institutions and hierarchies of the economy were transformed. And in the state, there was also a defining change. The society went from a sort of a messed up fledgling bourgeois democracy to a one-party, and in time even largely one-person, dictatorship. So it was a revolution, but the thing that was junked wasn't very developed either. And in the kinship sphere were there likely any changes?

Oh, yeah.

And what kind of changes?

All the structures that would've advanced you at one time, due to the economic and political change, would have become obstacles and things would've reversed.

Yes, regarding class and politics, that seems broadly correct to me as well. A new accommodation would be required and would lead to some kinship changes, at the least. It would be the case, that is, that the parts of the kinship sphere that were in tune with political and economic requirements from the past, requirements that were now gone, would have to alter. We know, for example, that at least the parts of the kinship sphere that had to do with creating capitalist mentality had to change because there were now no capitalist roles to manifest that precise mentality. If it didn't change, what would have happened? The people nurtured by kinship to have capitalist expectations and agendas wouldn't have fit the available political and economic slots. That would mean instability and turmoil, at least for a while, as things came into accommodation. But there are other aspects that might change. Suppose in the political sphere a dominant political perspective, Marxism-Leninism, becomes the basis for government. And suppose it turns out that that dominant political perspective is associated with a particular community, the Russian community, as compared to all sorts of other communities in the Soviet Union. What do you expect to happen in the community sphere as a result? Well, if it's going to accommodate, and our theory suggests it will, what has to happen?

It has to change.

But how? Suppose previously the various communities were either in some parallel condition of equality or maybe the Georgian community was dominant, or something (I actually have no idea what the situation was). Now in the new setting this would be a contradiction. That would be a problem. If the Georgian community was dominant in the prior cultural definitions, and the Russian community began running a dictatorial state, that would be a problem. People's expectations and adaptations—their consciousness and behavior as promoted by these two central facets of their lives— would be at odds. So you'd expect to see at a minimum an accommodation of hierarchies. You're going to see those things line up in accord with each other so that everybody isn't being compelled by different central features of society to do *a* and to *b*, where *a* and *b* are contradictory. You see what I'm saying? You can't be made a capitalist by your socialization, your upbringing, and your family when there's no capitalist role to fill. You can't be told by your entire culture that you're the dominant superior culture, and then you're subordinate to Russians in the state. And you can't be told by the state that you're the dominant group that should view itself as superior, and then you go over to the realm of community life and your culture is denigrated. This can't happen and have the society remain stable. So instead, when the dust settles, there will be some kind of accommodation.

And the thing to notice is that in all this muddling around that we are doing, this conceptualizing, we are actually making progress. We have a picture of revolution and evolution. This is theory building.

Let's take an example. Suppose somebody comes along and invents a birth control pill. First of all, why do they invent the birth control pill? We don't know, but what's a possible reason? To make a lot of money, let's say. So suppose they do it for profit and they don't give a damn about population or feminism. They do it for profit because the kind of economy we have makes profit a driving economic motivation. So they invent a birth control pill to make profits. Now, what happens in the rest of society? Does it have any other effects? Birth control can have rather profound effects over in the kinship sphere. It is not a small thing, this little technology, even though it's sort of an accidental phenomenon from the point of view of kinship, having arisen with entirely other purposes in mind. It didn't arise out of kinship dynamics and agendas. It arose out of the fact that somebody happened to discover the drugs and tried to make a buck off it. Yet over in kinship it might create social turmoil. That's possible. So that's one of the ways that dramatic things can happen.

Or, for instance, World War II comes along, the economy needs women and employs them, no longer asserting they are incapable of the various jobs they now must do. The state needs soldiers and gobbles up Black youth, but on the field of battle you can't have silly racist presuppositions mucking up communication, so racism begins to diminish and people's expectations about themselves alter.

Okay, so what's missing? We've got this little tool box much like a doctor has a medicine bag. If I am a doctor, I've got this bag with all these tools and I use them in my profession. We're doing social theory and trying to understand the world and we too have a tool box, a conceptual tool box, and it behooves us to use it. If we use it and it doesn't work, we can put something else in it or change something that's already in it. We might even have to get a new tool box, if it proves really flawed. But if all we do is reflexively answer questions that arise about society based on our intuitions, then the tool box isn't worth anything. It is only for show. Okay, our tool box has all these various concepts in it: people, human nature, all the attributes of people, the center; the various groups that emerge, whether they be classes or gender groups, races, etc.; the institutions with role structures; the four spheres of social life; the notion of accommodation, of co-definition, of co-reproduction. These are all concepts in our intellectual tool box. We have these concepts that we can use to perceive and think about society and history, hopefully more clearly than if we just used our unguided intuitions. And we now also have the concept revolution and the concept evolution. What's missing? Are we ready to specifically examine actual societies? Are we ready to go on out into the world and do our thing with our concepts? Or have we left something important out?

Think about that for next chapter, and try and explore the points raised so far. Try to do some applications of it.

6. Society and Its Context

An hour's listening disclosed the fanatical intolerance of minds sealed against new ideas, new facts, new feelings, new attitudes, new hints at ways to live. They denounced books they had never read, people they had never known, ideas they could never understand, and doctrines whose names they could not pronounce. Communism, instead of making them leap forward with fire in their hearts to become masters of ideas and life, had frozen them at an even lower level of ignorance than had been theirs before they met Communism.

–Richard Wright

Let's see. We left off last time with me asking if we were missing any critical concepts that we might want to highlight in order to understand history and society. We have people and the human center; and institutions and the institutional boundary; roles; four spheres; the defining features of each sphere; evolution and revolution; accommodation and co-definition; and even co-reproduction. What's missing?

Consciousness?

That's in the mix as human nature and the consciousness of people—it is an element of that concept, already included.

Remember when we said all the way back in the beginning that people were going to be a concept? We then also included their consciousness, goals, desires, skills, knowledge, etc. So we have consciousness. We need it and we have it. Anything else?

Environment. I said it earlier, but—

Indeed. But since then I have focused so much on all the other concepts, environment might have drifted out of your head. It probably did drift out of some people's attention, didn't it? That's what happens sometimes. In other words, the problem with theory is that once you've got one, it's possible to become dogmatic. You may think you've got a perfect theory, and since you've got a perfect theory, you don't have to worry about anything other than what it prioritizes. The person over there is complaining, "Wait! Wait! You left out birds, trees, pollution—you left it all out." But no, it's no matter. Your perfect theory is perfect, so he should just stop his whining and get out of your face. You've got a perfect theory, so you can't possibly have left out anything of consequence and, therefore, whatever that person is screaming about can't matter much. "Wait, I can't quite hear; whatever it is she's saying—remove her."

Of course this isn't the best way to be. The better approach is to pay attention to reality and especially to continually arising claims about reality that conflict with your views, because your theory may not be so perfect.

So we have gotten this far and what we have seems pretty good, except that there's no ecology. And there's another big thing missing also. We've got society. Ecology is missing, and something else major is missing as well.

The rest of the world?

Yes. We're missing international relations. We're missing the whole domain of foreign policy. We don't have a concept for it. It turns out that these flaws aren't a calamity, however. We don't have to start over in disgust because both of those missing concepts are a little different from what we have incorporated so far and they can now be added to what we have without calling our whole undertaking into question. Both are a little different than the other four spheres, for example, and given the way we approached the issues at hand, we just hadn't come to them yet.

Ecology isn't really a function that humans undertake, so it's dissimilar to the economy or polity, in that respect. Rather, it's the context in which humans undertake anything at all. It's the context in which a society exists. That doesn't mean ecology is unimportant. It's the table on which society is set. So it's profoundly important. And especially since it is affected by and affects everything that we have talked about so far, we have to have concepts that keep ecology in our field of concern. So we have to add ecology to the concepts that we so far have at our disposal. And we have to recognize that ecology sets limits. What kind of limits? Well, resources, weather—all sorts of limits on what a society can be. And in turn society can affect ecology, using it up, altering its shape and opportunity to thrive.

And for international relations, something similar holds. There isn't one society. If there were only one society, we wouldn't need concepts addressing international relations. But because there are other societies we must have concepts that highlight their interrelations. And then we have to deal with all sorts of phenomena that we're not going to deal with now, simply for want of time and space, such as trade or war or imperialism or colonialism.

Can't you make the argument, though, that the ecology is another sphere?

You could make the argument, if you wish to. Anyone can make any argument, explore any definition. I mean that sincerely. I'm not trying to brush the suggestion off. We define, that is, we pick out concepts however we like, as long as we are consistent and truthful to reality. However, we can't say a sphere of social life is determined by a basic function that has to be socially fulfilled in all societies, and then apply the label "sphere" to some part of reality that does not fulfill any social function. Also, when we use our concepts and see if we are getting useful and instructive results, we have to judge whether the way we have divided reality into component parts was a good choice. We may want to redefine or augment our definitions. Can anybody think of another thing we might want to make it's own sphere, even with sphere defined as it is now?

We say human beings are such that they must collectively undertake certain functions in societies: procreation and socialization, production, identity, adjudication. So now we've got four domains or spheres of life that people come together and create social institutions for. Suppose we try for another function that entails a fifth sphere. How about thinking as that function?

You mean the fact that people think—but what institutions does that require?

Well, it's something you could propose and then investigate to see the merit. People do inevitably think and so it is an inevitable part of all societies. And people do it together with communication and interaction. So in that respect we have the basis for considering whether it defines a social sphere. Now as you rightly ask, "Are there institutions associated with thinking?" Well, I don't know. Perhaps there are and we haven't noticed because we haven't been attuned to them, haven't had the categories, the concepts, that would highlight or even reveal them. So we'd have to investigate that. Maybe there are, but if so they are subtle and they haven't become part of our normal ways of seeing reality. Perhaps there are roles associated with thinking, but we aren't yet aware of them and haven't given them labels and thought about their relations. That happens in theory; sometimes we come across something quite new. Think of atoms, say, or quarks. These are concepts that were introduced long before anyone had any tangible evidence on behalf of the thing they were labeling, much less a common sense feel for the things labeled. The elaboration of other concepts and various scientists' examinations of the interrelations led them to expect to find these new (and for many others, unexpected) features in reality. Similarly, the elaboration of the idea of spheres of social life and human nature might lead someone to expect to find roles for thinking. So that kind of intuition or prediction can arise, and then it might be found true or false. Maybe there is something about how we think, and how we interact due to our thinking, that constitutes thinking roles that different people fulfill in relation to one another and their thought processes that constitute institutions. Are there dynamics associated with thinking? Maybe sectarianism is one. And so one could try to pursue this line of analysis and maybe it makes sense to do so. Are there different groups defined by the institutions associated with thinking? Perhaps there is the confident thinker and the nervous thinker, or something like that, or even different psychological states. I am not compelled by these musings that we need to follow this path for our purposes, though someone else might need to pursue some such thing for different purposes, or might need something far more elaborate (such as psychology, for example). So I could be wrong, and this new sphere could be critical for political activism.

But the key thing is that you see how the process of considering new concepts unfolds. And that said, let's return to our own unfolding process. Obviously ecology is not a set of institutions based on needing social roles to fulfill a necessary human function. We have an ecology even if we have no humans at all. So at this point, if we really want to consider seeing ecology as a sphere of social life, we would have to change the way we define sphere of social life so that ecology becomes one too. But I don't want to do that. I like the concept of a social sphere as it is. It seems useful and user-friendly to me. But suppose someone else does make a change. What happens? Well, then we've got two competing perspectives. It may be that one is just inconsistent and doesn't correspond to reality. Or it may be that both of them are valid, but one organizes its content more use-fully than the other does for directing our attention and our thoughts. If ecology as a social sphere with a new definition for what a social sphere is works better then my approach, I'm jumping ship to the new formulation. If my way works better, the advocate of the new scheme should jump ship back in my direction. Sometimes ego gets in the way of people moving toward what works best, but moving toward what works best is how we ought to proceed.

But the environment, as you say, does underlie everything. So don't we need to give it the same importance as kinship or economics, and thus elevate it to being a sphere?

Yes, ecology impacts everything, but why does that imply it has to be treated just as something else that also impacts everything? We haven't said that only social spheres are important, that only social spheres impact all sides of life. So the fact that ecology affects all life doesn't tell us that ecology has to be another social sphere. The fact that we realize it is important doesn't mean we have to group it with everything else that we find important. Likewise, it doesn't follow that if we don't call ecology a social sphere, we thereby indicate it is unimportant.

The fact that ecology is crucially important is precisely why I am suggesting that we understand it as the interactive and dynamic context in which all social life exists. But you're thinking that I have thus placed the environment in some kind of subordinate position, as compared to calling it another sphere, as you propose. But I said that there are four spheres. They compose society and help us understand the way society creates critical groups of people. But society isn't everything. There is something bigger. Maybe we need a word for society plus ecology. But I did say that the ecology provides the context for societies. In that respect it is obviously profoundly impor-tant. So the difference is not a question of importance. It's just a question of what direction to see things from, of how to group concepts in order to be as accurate and constructive and useful for our particular purposes as possible. I don't think ecology yields the kind of differentiation of social groups that the social spheres do, though of course a vegan might suggest that it does yield a hierarchy with humans on top and animals below.

Exactly. Why isn't that the hierarchy that the ecology's structure creates, or the ecology as we know it now, anyhow—one with humans on top?

So you might say, "Hold on a minute. You're making a mistake. The ecology does demarcate groups. There are roles in the ecology. Different species have different rights and privileges, and so this has to be a part of our social focus." And you might back up a step, then, and redefine a sphere to be a domain in which any one or more species collectively pursues functions centrally bearing on and essential to their life prospects. Now there is consistency. The social spheres we identified are such because within them humans pursue functions essential to their life prospects. The ecology becomes a sphere, you might argue, due to functions that are more general and that apply to all life. Okay, someone can follow that path consistently and it may be better. It will provide a framework that contains ecology as well as societies, but now instead of context, ecology could be called a fifth sphere. Is this better or worse? Are we going to see ecology more usefully and clearly, and likewise the other aspects, if we think of ecology analogously to the economy or polity or culture or kinship, or rather if we think of it as the context in which these develop, with rather different logic and features? I think the latter is the case. Someone else may think the former is the case. Utility for our purposes and practice will ultimately show us relative accuracy regarding what is really out there.

In essence, confronted by this suggestion, I just throw up my hands and say that I don't buy that it is going to be helpful to look at ecology in this newly proposed way, with society encompassing all living things, and so on. But I could just be mired in old ways of thinking. My intuitions, however strongly I may feel them, could be ignorant. You may say that the ecology does have roles. And you may even say the function at the base of ecology, which ecology exists to accomplish, is something like creating habitat, which is something all life forms do in order to survive. And you may argue that creating habitat or ecological niches does involve what we can usefully think of as institutional structures (based on roles that species fulfill in their habitats) that we can conceptualize as we conceptualize the economy or kinship sphere, the polity or culture. And, likewise, you might add that the ecology is key to social struggle, neither as a context for societies (which is what I want to call it) nor as something that we affect and which in turn affects us (which is what I want to say), but because of its own internal logic and morality. So the groups demarcated by ecology are humans and other species. And you could say that there's some kind of struggle, or whatever, among these. In that case, you might argue that it makes sense to have ecology as a social sphere because we should be treating it the same way that we're treating the other four spheres. I am not convinced. I think it will lead to viewing things that are different as though they are alike, and to missing their special differences, as a result.

But so far you have defined institution as a human creation.

Yes, I have, and so if we wanted to get ecology onto the map in the same logical category—social sphere—we'd have to change that element of our definition along with those that I've already mentioned, and no doubt others, too. If we don't want to do all that, if we think ecology is rather different and that saying it is similar wouldn't orient us usefully, then we can stick with the formulation as it already is developing and add this new feature or reality, the ecology, as the context within which societies develop rather than as another social sphere. That makes sense to me, so it's what I am going to do, but those of you who see this differently can do something different. And maybe it will turn out that I am only being dogmatic and clinging to my old conception rather than changing it in light of new evidence, and so in time your different approach will prove better. Or maybe it will turn out you are muddying differences due to wanting the neatness of five rather than four spheres.

The methodological point, however, which is why I am spending so long on this, is that we try to use our insights, intuitions, experience, guesses, or anything else at our disposal, to develop useful concepts. Then we look at reality using the concepts to try to explain, predict, and guide intervention in events to see whether the concepts we are proposing correspond to things as they are and also point us in useful directions for understanding, predicting, and intervening. If they do have that effect, that's good. If they instead distort our view, don't help us get a full picture regarding what we are interested in accomplishing, or are particularly hard to use, then we have to go back and start anew. So you can see that our difference in how to incorporate ecology isn't really over the approach to conceptualizing; it is over how best to pay attention to what's out there.

How to draw all those lines.

Exactly right. There is this interwoven tapestry of a world. And we draw these lines demarcating off parts, or concepts, to highlight components so that from the immense totality—which is way too much to keep entirely in mind—we can focus on what matters to us. The concepts highlight what we want to pay priority attention to as we try to discern relations and causes and possibilities. We draw boundaries defining concepts to organize our perceptions and thoughts, and once we have established our concepts we try to discern the non-obvious but nonetheless important relations that hold among them. That is what theory is all about.

Do we have a definition of ecology? I thought I knew what it was but maybe I don't.

Well, if by that you mean, "Could we have a definition of ecology?" my reaction is okay, let's define ecology. If you ask, "What do people mean by ecology?" then we have to see what they mean by ecology.

How do I consider it?

It seems to me that humans didn't create the ecology. We created everything else we have been highlighting: polity, kinship, institutions more generally, and so on. And we certainly helped induce many of the changes the ecology goes through, by our pollution, and so on. One possible answer is that ecology is simply everything (or perhaps everything alive) that's not either human or a conscious human artifact. So it isn't our buildings, and it isn't us, but it is bacteria, and flowers, and streams, the weather, and so on. Alternatively, some people may say that it's the natural stuff. That's of course a rather silly definition unless you really want to say that it's everything, because everything is natural. But if you use the term ecology to be everything, then what you're really doing is you're saying, "Okay, what we've called society plus something else is the ecology, which is everything. Now what's that 'something else?'" Maybe we will call the something else the environment. Then you would have the concepts society, environment, and ecology, with ecology being the sum total of society and environment. The labels are just what we name things. In this case, regardless of the specific names, we know what we are talking about.

7. Other Theories

I want to change gears a little now, if that's okay. Or perhaps I should say I want to look at this same issue of how we decide what lines to draw, what to label, and what names to use for our labels, from another direction. So, someone please tell me, what is the implication of Marxism as an injunction about what you should do? What's the strategic implication of Marxism?

Possibly you have to engage in class struggle?

Yes. And suppose that you think race has really important impact on human prospects, but you are a Marxist. What do you do?

You frame your attention to race in terms of class struggle.

Exactly, and so you unite and fight. You address race issues with great energy, but always in context of the implications for class struggle. And you do this not because you think race is unimportant in its own right—you may think it is currently paramount—but because your framework tells you that pursuing class struggle is the way to end the race problem too. So you see the issue of race in terms of how it affects and is affected by class relations and class conflicts. Okay, so what's the implication if you examine society and begin to feel that gender and economy are co-reproducing?

Socialist-feminism?

Indeed, because you have come to think that the kinship sphere and the economy both emit powerful influences affecting all sides of life, and also causing each to reproduce the other's defining features. And what do you address with great priority in that case? Kinship and the economy. And notice that the socialist-feminist claims this about any society even before looking at that society. It's a subtle point here. It's like having a theory that says all molecules will have some property. If someone comes along and says that yesterday we synthesized a new molecule, then the theorist who believes in the universality of the property will say, "And of course it had such and such a property," without even having looked to see.

The framework we've been developing for ourselves here, however, is different. We're saying that in any society we need to look at all four of the spheres because we don't know a priori anything more than that they will all be there, they will all impact one another, and they will all create social groups. So we need to look at all four to see if there is any prioritization, or whatever else we may find. We need to check what the basic institutions are for each sphere, and to examine the social groups and their various typical consciousness attributes, their levels of fulfillment and desire. We need to determine what's accommodating and what's co-defining and what's co-reproducing in the relations between the spheres. And we then need to ask which spheres are defining social life and social prospects and also which ones are co-reproducing each other's defining features? And those will be the ones we aim our strategies at. Okay, now, if we do that with the U.S., what do we come up? In other words, what do we say about the U.S. as compared to what the Marxist says or the socialist-feminist says?

All the above.

You intuit that that's the right answer for the U.S.?

Or the answer you're looking for.

Well, I want to hear what you think.

No, personally, I—given a capitalist system—I'd maybe say class. But that's my own personal bias.

It's not a bias; it's an opinion. Using our framework if it turned out that we analyzed the four spheres in the U.S. and we discovered that if we focus on the economy we have the best prospects for transforming the economy and also transforming everything else, then I would say we should focus there too. But if we look at the U.S. and we see instead that due to the relations between the spheres, even to transform the economy, and certainly to transform everything else, we need to have a more multiple focus, then I would favor a conceptual framework that is broader, such as ours. So there is a real choice to make, based on our best judgment about how society is structured, how it preserves and reproduces itself, and what implications our actions are likely to have. But one major difference is that some frameworks make this choice a priori, opting for economy, or polity, or kinship, or culture alone as central for all societies, even before looking. I think that is a mistake.

But you believe that the capitalist system is profoundly powerful, right? And that class structure is powerful. It's so powerful that it probably affects gender, race, and the state. Not one-way causal or anything, right? But it really does affect all those things.

Sure it does. Yes, I know that's true in our society, and in every capitalist society, as a matter of fact. And we can even usefully ask how the economy affects all those other aspects. And in our framework we expect that the answer will be that it extends out its influence and affects their ordering of people in hierarchies, and that it also perhaps affects their very definition. In other words, the influence of the economy may reconstruct how other spheres are organized, to some degree, so that the other spheres don't just accord with but even re-create the class system as well as their own underlying hierarchies. And then we could look to see the actual details of how all this occurs, in our society, say.

Yes, in the U.S. the economy pushes families and religions and everything else, so they too become class defined. I think so.

I agree, but then why don't you want to take that into account in your practice? The stronger you believe that the economy impacts the definition of other spheres to make them reproduce class relations, the more multifold your approach needs to be even if you are only interested in altering class relations.

We made this case earlier. If the economy is powerfully influential, then just to transform class relations, at least permanently, you may well have to also deal with all the other spheres with the same level of attention as you deal with the economy because they're also reproducing class relations, which is the thing you want to deal with. But even though you would want to address all the spheres, if you thought the economy was most influential, you might still be prioritizing class issues while doing so.

On the other hand, when I look at the U.S. it does seem to me that not just one sphere but instead each of the four spheres is powerfully defining the quality of our lives. It isn't that one of them is defining the quality of our lives and the other three are largely an outgrowth of that. It seems instead, that each of them has powerful effects on what is possible for a human being to be. And more controversially, they all seem to me to be reproducing each other. Culture is reproducing class, gender, and political relations. The polity is reproducing gender, cultural, and class relations. And it isn't just that they're each doing this a little bit, but that they're each doing it profoundly. And also it seems to me that the divisions into groups that each sphere causes are all critical—not only one or another of them—in determining how people see society and develop personal and group interests and agendas, so it makes sense to focus on all four of these spheres and their social relations rather than prioritizing any one. Not everything in the universe needs to always be equally prioritized, but it seems to me that all four social spheres are centrally reproducing the kinds of oppressions that we want to overcome and therefore each should be centrally addressed to maximize our chances to eliminate these oppressions.

So, just supposing for a minute that we all come to accept a view like that, after more specifically examining our own societies, what would it tell us we need to do in our societies?

Well, we need some kind of strategic approach that is multi-focused and we need a vision that addresses all four spheres. Because if we don't change one or another of them it might bring us back into the old decay we suffered before. So we need a vision for all four spheres and we need a strategy that's going to address them all. First, who's going to be in motion in each sphere? Who's going to be the agent of change?

The most oppressed.

Why only the most oppressed? The most oppressed would be in motion, yes; that makes sense. But why only the most oppressed? Who else could it be? Take the economy, for example.

I think the most oppressed would be the most likely to rebel.

Okay, but what about in the economy?

Well it could be anyone other than the most rewarded.

Yes. And it might be at a particular point in time that somebody other than those at the top or at the bottom is really aroused and fights hard and makes a change. And does what?

Takes control.

Makes themselves the new ruling class, and then what happens at the bottom?

They're still at the bottom.

Yes, that might occur and, indeed, I think that does occur in an economic revolution in which what I call the coordinator class becomes the ruling class. It's certainly logically possible. So we have to look and see whether it happens in history. And lo and behold, there it is all over the place, once we have the eyes to see it. If we don't have the lenses to see it with, then we may miss it, certainly. In that case we'll just call whatever overthrows capitalism, socialism, and all of a sudden we'll think it's the end of class oppression, because what else could it be, after all. And if we are wedded enough to that conception, for whatever reason, then we won't see all the overwhelming contrary evidence. Indeed the power of concepts is remarkable. If we only have class concepts based on ownership relations, for example, then we look at post-capitalist economies and we call them socialism because private ownership is gone, and with it the capitalists. So what else could the new system be? Our only available concepts are capitalism and socialism. If it isn't capitalism, then we can conclude it must be socialism. And amazingly, yet predictably, if we start calling it socialism and if, later, for whatever reasons, we come to the revelation that, well, it isn't socialism after all, what will we most likely do? We will go back to calling it capitalism, or maybe deformed capitalism, or state capitalism. What we lack is another term entirely.

Capitalists are removed, private property is gone, workers still are subordinate (now to managers, planners, and what we call coordinator class members) and some folks act as though it is still capitalism because they don't like it, so then it can't be socialism, so by default it must still be capitalism. And other folks alternatively call it socialism, seeing that it obviously isn't capitalism (because there is no private ownership of the means of production) but lacking any other concept to apply. It doesn't matter that workers have no power, they still call it socialism. They are blind to why it isn't. This reveals how a conceptual framework can narrow the possible perceptions and thoughts people are able to arrive at. The discussion is a sidebar from our agenda, but it's instructive about any theoretical agenda's possible pitfalls. The people at the top in the Soviet Union called it socialism as well. Why?

To legitimate it.

Indeed, the people who ran the Soviet Union didn't think they had a workers' paradise. That's ridiculous. They knew otherwise, obviously, as did everyone living in the country. But they did know that if they called it a workers' paradise, socialism, it would be much harder to rebel against. If they said that their economy was the best possible economy that workers could have and that the only other thing they could have was Appalachia or Harlem, then Russian workers would be more willing to stick with their system.

And what did elites in the U.S. call our system? Well, they called it democracy and freedom and all the rest. Do the people at the top think that everybody is enjoying real democracy? No, they're not that dumb. They know they are in control. But they call it all those things and then they say there's nothing else that people can aspire to other than dictatorship. And then it is hard for critics to justify rebellion.

But we can already get beyond these faults because we have concepts that provide more insight than that. Not resting on our laurels, however, how do we make what we have even better?

One thing is that we have to enrich our concepts for understanding the interrelations among institutions and behaviors central to each of the four spheres, for understanding consciousness, and for understanding people's alliances and histories. Okay, where do we go to do that?

We can keep developing our concepts ourselves, independent of past efforts. Or if we want to improve our conceptualization of the polity, maybe we should go to the anarchist heritage and look for additional useful concepts and analyses there. And to enrich our gender concepts maybe we should go to the feminist heritage. And for race maybe we should go to the nationalist heritage. And for the economy maybe we should go the Marxist heritage. My own view is we can pursue the first three agendas confidently, but we have to be very cautious about the fourth. Let's see why.

We know that when consulting feminism we're consulting a heritage which is going to lack, for example, a really good understanding of how the economy, the polity, and the culture impact kinship. It will probably be highly explanatory in the other direction, kinship affecting the rest of society, but it won't be near as explanatory regarding impacts on kinship because it presupposes the dominance of kinship and denigrates looking at other spheres' influences back upon kinship. So when we consult the feminist tool box to add new concepts to those we've been developing, we expect we will need to do some adapting because the heritage underestimates the degree of mutual effect. And the same goes for going to the other heritages—anarchism, Marxism, nationalism—each of which also underestimates mutual effect.

But if that's the only big problem with these heritages, then we can take the problem into account when we examine their concepts and can adapt and refine them to add them to our tools. This is true for three of the schools of thought—feminism, anarchism, and nationalism—I think, largely because these three each understand and conceptualize their focused sphere from the perspective of a most oppressed group, which is our priority too: to liberate the oppressed.

However, regarding Marxism, I don't think this claim is true. Marxism is a theory of the economy. It is anti-capitalist, so it's not just a rationalization for what's out there, which is of course good. But I think it shines its light from the perspective of advancing the interests of what I call the coordinator class, not the working class. In other words, Marxism addresses economies guided by the agenda of people who monopolize knowledge, information, and access to levers of power: people who exist, in capitalist economies, in a space between labor and capital. This coordinator class is subordinate to capital and works, at least in part, to attain leverage and power independent of capitalist interests and on behalf of its own enrichment. And the coordinator class is above labor, often administrating it, defining its options, and manipulating or governing it. So if Marxism is elaborated from the perspective of or in light of the agenda and interests of the coordinator class, then we would expect not only that Marxism would be narrow in ways analogous to feminism, anarchism, and nationalism, but also that it would be flawed regarding the economy itself, and in quite important and basic ways.

And, indeed, that is what I think I find when I examine Marxism closely. I find that Marxism has the wrong class analysis, emphasizing ownership but essentially ignoring power differences other than those rooted in property relations—including those that result from role definitions in the division of labor itself. Marxism certainly understands much about capitalism, but it makes some fundamental mistakes as well, mainly hiding the relation between coordinators and capitalists and especially between coordinators and workers, and therefore missing elements of oppression that derive from subordination to coordinators. So conceptually, we have to not just borrow from the Marxist heritage, and not even just enrich the Marxist heritage to more fully incorporate the impact of other spheres (as we have to do with feminism, nationalism, and anarchism), but we have to overhaul Marxism considerably to correct its class analysis and get the associated concepts right. And indeed, it seems to me that we have to overhaul it so much, that the result is no longer in any real sense Marxism.

I want to go back....What do you mean by radical nationalism?

Well, I think it refers to all sorts of national or community-focused perspectives that don't take sufficient account of other domains. Many Black activists in the U.S., for example, are more attuned to looking at the world with cultural concepts than with any others. Some favor a kind of amalgam; for example, Marxist nationalists, focus on economics and community rather than only community. It's not that a radical nationalist doesn't think gender is important. She may or may not. But she will certainly think that culture is more strategically central. Many activists in the Black community have a more or less nationalist orientation in which they think culture is the defining factor. So just as is the case with radical feminists or orthodox Marxists, they too put more emphasis on one domain than on the others. Activists then see events differently— O.J. Simpson's trial, for example, or affirmative action, or war—depending on which framework they hold.

But to return to evaluating Marxism, and to also stay in touch with your query, what's the Marxist vision or goal for culture? Does anybody know? Maybe you can guess.

Class culture?

Okay, you are using the concepts we are developing, which is good. But what does that mean? What does it mean for Georgian culture, Moslem culture, Russian culture, or Jewish culture? It homogenizes them. That's one possibility and you can see how it logically emerges.

Suppose the economy appears to you to be the dominant factor in society and history, and class appears to you to be the dominant grouping of people. Your aim will be to have the working class (or perhaps the coordinator class) rise in power, and this will impact how you relate to all other problems in society. If that's what you believe, then most likely what you want culturally will be whatever you deem to be the right culture: socialist culture, you might call it. You want the correct culture to accord with your preferred class aims. You want a culture that's consistent with the economy that you're trying to create. It isn't an inevitable choice, but it is the obvious one, and the historical one. You aren't highly attuned to the nuances or even many main defining realities of culture. You know your own culture. You like it. What the hell, why shouldn't everyone share it with you, one nice big culture?

But this choice is of course a nightmare for most culturally or community-based groups, which is why most culturally or community-based groups don't relate positively to Marxism. It's why most indigenous communities worry about Marxism. They see it as auguring a future in which their religious, ethnic, or other identity will be subsumed into the one culture of the dominant community on the grounds of attaining a preferred socialist identity. That's why among indigenous Indians in the U.S., or anywhere in the world, there are very few Marxists. They're hostile to Marxism because they intuit that if Marxism wins, diverse cultures are gone. Even though Marxists say they want to protect and liberate Indians, Indians hear it as Marxists wanting to protect and liberate Indians around matters of class—protect Indians as people, but don't protect Indians as Indians. That's just not a Marxist concept.

Not all Marxists have views like this...

That's quite true. Not all people who consider themselves Marxists will think this way, but in practice, and history does show this very clearly, that's what the overall orientation becomes even against the best sympathies and insights of many practitioners. And there's a reason that happens, and it is actually a reason Marxists understand in other contexts. It's because the conceptual tool box pushes so hard in those directions, and so does what's won at each new stage of struggle. Of course each individual is a unique entity with various views and desires; this is true for Marxists, feminists, anarchists, or nationalists. But with any of these orientations, all the involved individuals are using an apparatus and a vision that has implications of its own. Which will have more impact—the disparate goodwill of some actors, or the shared bias of the overall framework? Most often the latter will dominate in average overall outcomes, repeating as it does from person to person, so that each of these groups, if the narrowness of its focus isn't corrected, will have problematic aims analogous to the above example.

In other words, most often the apparatus that's being used by all the advocates of a narrow perspective, even if not always entirely consistently, is going to overwhelm the idiosyncrasies and different experiences they each have, at least on average. So there are many Marxists who have sincerely wanted multiple cultures to attain mutually respectful dignity, of course. But in Marxist movements and particularly in societies that Marxists have built, this hasn't happened. Why? Because the overall impact of the framework, even against the wills of many of its practitioners, is to rule that result out, elevating instead the cultures of the new elite. And the same occurs with nationalists having inadequate vision around economy, or feminists around polity, and so on. This is what we try to correct via taking concepts from each framework and refining them in light of our fourfold rather than singular orientation.

But more damning, while many Marxists sincerely want workers to rule their own lives, nonetheless, the result of Marxist movements winning change is that workers don't rule their own lives. The conceptual tool box and the class interests and structural choices of Marxist movements as a whole, even against the sincere and contrary desires of many of their rank and file members, have always had as their guiding logic to advance the interests of another class, the coordinator class. And so it is mainly this other class and not workers that rises to power with Marxist victories, even despite the contrary hopes of particular members. Russia certainly had decentralized movements of workers developing their own organic institutions to take over their workplaces. But that was destroyed by the Bolsheviks.

The revolution stopped.

No. That's not the way I would view it, although some people, including folks who I like a lot in many other respects, do talk about it that way. With our concepts, the revolution that won destroyed those grassroots attempts aimed at something entirely different. But it was a revolution that did that. It didn't stop; it won.

But what got trounced was the revolution.

No, what got trounced was a possible revolution, but not the only possible revolution. What won was a revolution also, because it changed the basic relations of the economy and society. What got trounced was a different agenda, but not the only revolutionary agenda.

But what won wasn't liberating. How can we call it a revolution?

Did we define revolution as something liberating? I don't remember doing that. I remember defining it as being a change in the basic defining relations of one or more spheres of society.

So here we are back at the same place again: asking how we should define our concepts. We can define the term revolution however we like, assuming we match it to something real. If we want a concept that highlights only big changes that we like, then we might say revolution is a change in a sphere of social life that liberates the worst off constituency. Or maybe we want a concept that refers to basic changes in defining institutions which reduce oppressions throughout society to some major extent (more than, say, the Russian revolution did). We could opt for that too. I just don't find these approaches very useful. To virtually everyone at the time throughout the world, the Russian revolution was certainly a revolution. Out goes capitalism. Out goes bourgeois democracy. In comes something else. It wasn't the revolution we favor because what replaced those old systems wasn't a new system we favor. But that is another matter. It is generally unwise to use familiar words in arcane ways, it seems to me. It makes for too much trouble communicating in public.

Another question that arises is whether we should use the word socialism for the kind of economy we want. Well, some people say yes, because to do otherwise would be a capitulation. But, what if it is stupid to use the word for our aims because the only thing that the word socialism connotes in most people's minds, like the only thing that the word communism connotes in most people's minds, is the system that was in the Eastern Bloc countries? So if you say I'm a socialist, it means to most people you're for the old East German economy and therefore you're not worthy of admiration or attention. Are we accomplishing something constructive by using words that have that implication? Maybe we are, for example, if we mean to defend the old East German economy as a valid model. But not otherwise.

I can't take the homogenized character of all this. It's bloodless.

You mean you don't like it—

I detest it.

It's giving you goose bumps.

It's worse than that because you're robbing humanity of every-thing that makes it interesting and you're reducing it to a bunch of automatons.

You may feel that I am somehow diminishing humanity, reducing it or homogenizing it, to say that the role structures around us have such profound effects on us, pushing us this way and that, as if we were a herd of cattle. But I'm not saying humans are some kind of infinitely malleable entity, perfectly and completely molded by social roles, each of us entering and then emerging alike. Humans, we have instead argued, are highly complex, highly individual creatures. The part of the equation that humanity brings to the table is very diverse, though of course there are also a great many things in common, innately, person to person.

On the other side of the table, society puts up institutions which we identify in the four spheres of social life, and it offers us the roles that you and I fill, which may be very similar or even effectively identical. But the fact that we both fill roles, perhaps even some of the same roles, doesn't mean we will be identical people. We each have lots of things, including our innate beings, contributing to what we do and think and feel, and this differs from you to me. But, to the extent that we occupy the same role slots in society, one factor that is powerfully affecting us will be largely the same for us. And if that factor is sometimes so powerful that for large numbers of people it will imbue many shared notions, beliefs, ideas, and behaviors, then we need to be aware of that.

Why doesn't it bother you that millions speak the same language, one language? It needn't be oppressive that we have commonalties and are affected by our shared conditions. It is the reality we live. The commonalties from role to role and institution to institution could be liberating, promote diversity, and so on, instead of being limiting and oppressive. And when the commonalities are oppressive, we can work to alter them, which, of course, is the whole point of the work we are doing.

Are we going to talk about how to achieve revolution?

Yes, but it might be worth noting that the framework that we're developing here doesn't necessarily have to be used by somebody who's revolutionary. Somebody could listen to this whole discussion and say, "Okay, now what? I like the theory; it seems powerful. But I also like what I see around me. I like the gender hierarchy. I like the race hierarchy. I like the economic hierarchy. I like the political hierarchy. I understand it pretty well now—how it all meshes and reproduces itself, how parts of it co-reproduce—and I'll just keep exploring and expanding my understanding of it, even while I support it."

In other words, using a theoretical framework doesn't mean that you have to value possibilities the same as everyone else who uses the same theory. I'd like to think that anybody who starts to do what we are doing would at least be progressive, but it's not necessarily the case.

But yes, we'll talk soon about what kinds of structures, activities, organizational forms, and goals, seem to make sense to attain revolutionary changes given our framework—about what kinds of behavior and interaction are needed to make a revolution across all four spheres.

How do you bring in the international aspects?

There are two pretty obvious ways we can extend what we are doing to a worldwide approach. We could take the whole world and say there are four spheres and so on, and look at it as a single entity. Now the whole world becomes a big society—which is reasonable enough and there are people have chosen to view it like this—and this whole world system has lots of cultural communities, economic components, and so on. With this approach in the world's community sphere there would be countries, probably. In other words, in this way of conceptualizing the whole world is one entity. It has community, culture, economics, etc. And the countries become communities within the whole world. But I don't choose to see things that way. Given my intuitions about what value the theory is likely to have for real people, I focus on societies and note that there are different societies each of which has instances of these attributes that we've been talking about, making them similar, and each of which also has singular and different aspects. They have much in common, especially if they have the basic defining features in common. And of course all of these societies exist in relation to each other. So in that latter regard, what can we expect?

We can expect that each of the societies by virtue of its particular set of institutions is going to have certain tendencies or drives in the international arena. Many people think the only sphere that impacts international aims is the economy. So the drives that emerge from within a society regarding the rest of the world, in this view, are to colonize it if possible to colonize, in the worst case, and the ensuing international relations are just an economic phenomenon. But I think a society's dispositions in the world arena are not just an economic phenomenon. If you look through history, it's often also in part a community phenomenon: a phenomenon of warring cultures. That doesn't mean there's not an economic dimension. Both are present. And remember the feminist who looks at General Motors and sees the family. She may also look at international relations and see powerful gender pressures at work in which men are basically fighting over female possessions. And if you look at the behaviors and you look at the phenomena, it's hard to say that that it isn't the case, or at least a significant factor, at least in some instances. And of course reasons of state play a large role, as well. All these dynamics are operative.

Now we might reasonably guess that in the international field in the modern world, at the current moment, the economic impetus from countries is perhaps the dominant one. If so, in understanding contemporary international relations, a considerable amount and perhaps a disproportionate amount of time should go to understanding how capitalism (the economic sphere) compels or impels economic activities outward toward other societies. But this should not be done exclusively, by any means. For example, you can make a case that Soviet involvement abroad has historically been more political than economic, in many cases. For instance, Eastern Europe did not enrich the Soviet Union. Eastern Europe was the Soviet Union's colony in many senses, but not simply due to some kind of economic logic. While the U.S. enriched itself off Central America, arguably the Soviet Union impoverished itself off Eastern Europe. Something different was occurring, profoundly different, in the two cases, except perhaps at the end of World War II when Stalin went in and ripped off the infrastructure in the iron curtain countries. But after that, the ongoing relation was an impoverishment of the Soviet Union, not an enrichment of it. So it's unlikely that there was solely an economic dynamic at work there, a dynamic of simple exploitation. And this indicates that things other than economics can be at work and can yield important international phenomena. So what you have to do is look at the situation and see what the situation is instead of just assuming an outcome without looking. And that is what our framework does a good job of promoting, I think.

I'd like to ask about revolution and evolution. If you have a strong enough and a sudden change in one facet, can the other facets then change by evolution. Or does it take more than one revolution to get all the spheres transformed?

If a sphere changes in its defining relations, for whatever reasons, by whatever process, it is a revolution. Suppose you're in a society in which all four spheres are co-reproducing each other very strongly. Each sphere, by its roles and dynamics, tends to reproduce the defining features of it and of the other three spheres as well. Revolutions in any sphere are always parts of long processes. They might involve tumultuous events near the end of the process, sure, but it's very rare that it isn't a process spread out over time. But suppose, in tune with your question, it's a tumultuous event, as you suggest, that comes largely out of the blue. So it's a tumultuous event and you get a change in one of those spheres and the other spheres don't change at that point. What happens next? Well, it depends. If the kind of change in the one sphere is such that the others can accommodate to it without disrupting themselves entirely, then you can have a revolution in the first sphere and slower changes in the other ones that thereby come into a stable accord with it. Perhaps the elimination of apartheid will prove to be this way, though getting rid of apartheid didn't happen overnight.

Or suppose you consider the Cuban revolution. They had a revolution primarily in the economy and the polity and then they made changes in their culture and their kinship sphere also, over time. All this stabilized into a new form and that was that. The changes in all the other spheres were pretty quick, relatively. But they didn't revolutionize, I think, in the liberatory sense. You haven't got liberated kinship. You haven't got liberated culture. And for that matter, you haven't got liberated economics or liberated politics. But you have gotten dramatically new forms of each, changes in defining relations—vastly better than what existed before—and therefore revolutions in those two spheres, at least, but not in the others, which still have the old structures.

Is Cuba a military regime? Is Cuba authoritarian? Do you think Fidel's a good guy?

Of course Cuba's government is authoritarian. Cuba's polity is a one-party dictatorship with a single dictator. Lots of leftists just can't bring themselves to say that. Now that's pretty strange to me. How can you not bring yourself to say what's obviously the case? It's like not bringing oneself to say that that blue thing out there is the ocean. But you can see in their difficulty in uttering the words the impact of biases and narrow concepts. You might want to debate about whether or not Castro is much more benevolent or much more insightful or much more wise or much more this or that than most other dictators, or than all other dictators, or even than most or perhaps all other elected leaders, say. But he's still a dictator. And Cuba doesn't have a form of government that I support.

It is interesting that if you go back and you look at Cuba and you read Fidel and Che in the early days of the revolution, you'll notice they started out fantastically hostile to the Communist Party and the Soviet Union and they espoused what arguably were the most libertarian and humane views for the economy and society that you're going to find in print anywhere from people who have attained that kind of position. But the constraints they faced in the world—the international context imposed by U.S. policies—were very powerful and the options at their disposal were therefore very limited. And when they got around to actually redesigning their economy, what were they supposed to do? What option did they have? Well, Che, the doctor, became head of the economy and his option was to go and open up a Polish or German or Czech or Soviet textbook, and start implementing the economy described there, because there was, as far as they could perceive, either that option or to succumb to Wall Street.

In tune with these questions, next chapter let's move on to address thinking about vision and strategy. It's not because we have done everything that needs doing regarding theory, of course. It's just to continue the process of getting an overarching picture of what steps are involved with all these tasks, so that later in exploring all these matters further we will to able to greatly enrich the limited results we have obtained here.

8. Thinking About Vision and Strategy

It's a poor sort of memory which only works backward.
                                                    –Cheshire Cat

And you, are you so forgetful of your past, is there no echo in your
soul of your poets' songs, your dreamers' dreams, your rebels' calls?
                                                    –Emma Goldman

The next couple of chapters are going to be very broad, dealing mostly
with vision and strategy, and a good accompaniment would be to
venture out onto the World Wide Web to some leftist sites and look
at their mission statements and particularly at their vision and
strategy statements, and assess them in light of what we have been
developing. You might usefully start at *Z Magazine*'s site, *ZNet*, which
is at http://www.zmag.org , at the section called Strategy and Vision.

So far we've got a domain of focus that we want to understand,
society and history, and we're looking at it and trying to find
elements within it most indicative of its features. We know good
concepts are ones that are well suited to our purposes, that we can use
flexibly, and that will counter biases we may have due to background.

Presumably, if we can become clear in our purposes, we can learn more about our concepts, refining and enriching them in light of our needs and experience. But so far we haven't said much about our purposes. Even if we don't care to engage in the struggle for change—and hopefully we do—vision and strategy are next on the conceptual agenda.

To further refine our views of society and history and to fill out our concepts for each of the four spheres and about the institutional center and the human boundary as well as the ecological and international context, we need to be clearer about what we want to accomplish with our theory. What project is our conceptual framework supposed to facilitate? Within what context are we trying to explain, predict, and intervene?

To understand what strategy is, think of a bridge. You are on one side. You want to be on the other side. The bridge has to be rooted at both ends. It's senseless to talk about strategy or getting from where we are to where we want to go if our proposals are suited to conditions on one side of that divide, but not the other. It's a trivial insight, but it is nonetheless important. If we have a strategy that orients nicely toward our goal but which makes wrong assumptions about where we are starting out, it will get us nowhere fast. On the other hand, if we have a strategy that understands the present context quite well, and that relates sensibly to its possibilities and has good proposals for moving rapidly forward, but that doesn't aim toward where we want to wind up, that might be worse than having no strategy at all. We'll move fast, but likely in the wrong direction.

I want to travel so I learn the getting going side of my trip—how to get a bus or plane schedule and how to pack my bags—in light of the way things are in the place I am embarking from. I learn various tactics associated with getting moving. But suppose I forget whether I want to go to San Francisco or New Orleans. So I take off well; I move quickly; however I wanted to see New Orleans, but I wind up in San Francisco. I need a destination and my bridge has to point to it. A six-year-old can understand this claim without difficulty. To have a sensible strategy you need to know where you want to go. Yet, however simple this insight may be, most leftists don't understand it, or at any rate, pay little attention to it. Most leftists function in terms of how to get things moving and ask repeatedly, "How do we get going? What do we want to move away from? How do we get something to happen? How do we move away from where we are now?" Leftists respect these questions, rightly, but for the most part wrongly ignore the question of destination: Where do we want to wind up?

What we need in a strategy is a kind of recipe of possible things that we might do, steps that we can choose from and cobble together to move forward depending on situations we encounter, but in a broadly understood pattern. And obviously the steps have to take us from where we are, and therefore they have to be true to the reality of where we are. Radicals generally understand that much, it seems. We can't make believe our present conditions are other than they are. We can't act as though conditions are better or worse than they are and expect to have useful impact. But our recipe of steps to take, able to account for changing conditions that we may encounter and able to move us away from our starting point by properly accounting for it, also has to point in the direction that we wish to go lest we wind up somewhere else entirely. What could be simpler to understand? Yet how many radicals can say much about where they want to wind up?

So to develop strategy we have to talk a little bit about where it is that we want to go. Given the conceptual tool box we've developed, how do we propose goals? How do we come up with a goal for society?

You'd look at society's role structures and its component parts and the four spheres and identify the problems that exist in those spheres and how you'd want them to look after a revolution.

Yes, you are using the concepts we have to address questions that we encounter. You might add, "Here are the values I want to have implemented in a good society, so I not only have to get role structures that get rid of the negatives I find around me, but I also have to incorporate these positive values that I desire." That's right. That's all there is to it.

So we look at the rightful functions of the four spheres and ask how we can accomplish these needed functions in ways consistent with our values. We first determine for each sphere what we want to attain, and we then think about institutions able to do it. Suppose we did that for kinship and we decided that marriage as an institution and mothering and fathering as sex-divided procreation and socialization roles were at the root of the production and reproduction of sexual hierarchy and patriarchy. If we decided that, which once upon a time some people in the women's movement believed, then in coming up with a goal we might reason, "Okay, what new institutions do we want to adopt that can attain whatever is good about marriage, but without the bad aspects? And what new institution do we want to adopt to accomplish the needed parts of procreation and socialization that female mothering and male fathering achieve, but again without the negative attributes, and, instead, fostering values we desire?" So, for instance, suppose we decide we want something called parenting, which we envision taking the place of mothering and fathering. We want a society in which there's no such thing as the mothering and fathering sex-divided roles, and there's just one role called parenting that's not sex divided, so that women and men have (with the exception only of breast feeding) no different behavioral responsibilities regarding upbringing.

We start to conceive a set of new roles and new structures and we thereby try to develop a vision for the kinship sphere. We try to answer the question of what we as feminists want at that institutional level. And then we'd have other questions to answer about the rest of society because any new kinship structures we envisioned could have different implications for the rest of society than the old ones did. No sexual division of labor could exist in the economy, for example, because if it did, it would conflict with the implications and requirements of our new kinship sphere. So we would examine these implications around the other spheres in some detail. And then we would have a vision for kinship. It wouldn't be a blueprint, but it would be a sufficiently complete conception so that if a normal human being asked us what we want instead, as we're so angry at sexism, we don't have to just throw up our hands or vaguely answer, "Justice." We would have a more compelling answer that could not only satisfy the questioner, but also give us a way to be positive about our aspirations, and perhaps most important, to orient our practice.

Or suppose we tried to do the same thing around the community sphere. We might begin by clarifying the needs of groups that identify themselves as communities as having a means of celebration and identity. Races, religions, and ethnic groups have legitimate needs for means of celebration and identity, and perhaps we conclude that that is what the community sphere's function is, and that these needs should be diverse and respected. Perhaps we find that it's the interrelations between these communities that are most often the problem. So we require a relationship among cultural communities that is more intercommunal and that defends any group that's a minority and guarantees its status against incursions from without. And then we develop an institutional picture of what it would be like to have a liberated community sphere that meets the legitimate functions of identity and celebration and cultural grounding in a way that propels values we favor. That is, we clarify what multiculturalism means institutionally or what intercommunalism means institutionally, or whatever word we might choose for our vision.

Or suppose we do it around politics. We first try to clarify what political functions society has—legislative, adjudicative, executive, and any others. We next determine positive values that we favor for political exchange and process. We try to define new institutions for arriving at shared norms for society, for deciding disputes and/or dealing with violations, and for developing shared programs and implementing them. We don't throw out the baby of needed political functions with the bath water of oppressive hierarchical government bureaucracy. Instead, we retain what's valid and needed in the political functions, but find ways to accomplish them that produce greater justice, truth, empowerment, participation, and whatever other values we aspire to.

Or what about envisioning a new economy? If we only pointed to the bad, we might point to private ownership in the means of production and we might simply urge a new kind of economy that doesn't have private ownership in the means of production but instead has what?

State ownership and central planning?

Yes, and if we did that, the economy we proposed would then have a coordinator class of planners and managers and other intellectual actors who would have a monopoly on knowledge and levers of power, still ruling over disempowered workers. So if we don't like that, then to be sure to get something worthy we might instead not only try to get rid of bad institutions, but also to very consciously attain desired new institutions. We might ask not only what we want to escape, but what we want to attain. Then we might come up with a different kind of economic vision. To convey a bit more feeling of how to think about vision, and how to come up with a vision for a part of life, I want to take the discussion of economic vision just a little further, not because it is more important, but just because I can speak more confidently about it. (If you want to take it a lot further by the way, you might consider the companion Arbeiter Ring volume to this one, *Thinking Forward*, which is entirely about economic vision.)

So we want to envision a new and better economy. In a nutshell, we look at the economic sphere and discern what economics is all about, which is conducting production, allocation, and consumption in tune with expressed desires and without squandering available resources and potentials. We then realize that we want an economy to accomplish that in a manner that advances our values. So we try to enumerate such values. We are drawn immediately to the need to have some positive aspiration regarding distribution—who gets what and why. And we know that an economy's roles affect the way people interrelate, so we want some positive value regarding human interrelations, too. Economics involves power and influence, and so we need to know what kind of distribution of power and influence we want. And finally, economics can homogenize or diversify, and we need a value there too.

So we start to think about these areas of concern and evaluation and we begin to evolve a set of values that economic activity should propel. So suppose we start with this: that is, an economy should promote diversity; it should foster solidarity; it should distribute income and circumstances so that people who exert more effort and sacrifice get more income, and those who exert less get less (unless there is an reason for not being able to exert, such as illness, and then folks get what they need); and an economy should apportion decision-making influence so that each person (or group) influences decisions in proportion as he or she (or it) is impacted by that decision. Elsewhere I have written a lot about these values and their merits. The last two are controversial, but suppose, nonetheless, that after thinking about them long and hard we settle on these values, or something similar to these. Then we have to examine economic institutions to find ways to get production, allocation, and consumption accomplished that enhance (rather than subvert) these values.

If we look at typical institutional choices—private ownership of the means of production and reward in the form of profit or payment to bargaining power, market allocation, central planning, and typical job definitions that give some people far more rewarding conditions of work and far more influence over outcomes than others—we find them all horribly wanting regarding impact on social relations, equity, and decision making. So we reject them and develop new institutions for a worthy vision.

Maybe we come up with balanced job complexes, for example, wherein each actor does a mix of tasks that are different from what others do but which, in total, have comparable quality of life and empowerment impact. And we come up with consumer and producer councils and democratic oversight of workplaces with self-managing decision-making methods. And we come up with a new allocation system that emphasizes horizontal communication and decision making (which we call participatory planning) and values items in tune with their true social costs and benefits. And we come up with remuneration norms that reward only effort and sacrifice, not power, property, or output, yet provide proper and workable incentives for productivity and innovation. So we do all that, we investigate it and develop it, and we see that it really does apportion income and circumstances and power and influence properly. We finally settle on a broad structural vision for a new economy. That's good. It gives us positive aims. It answers the question of what it is we want. It grounds our critiques. It sensitizes us to the limitations of some critical approaches that rightly attack current ills but don't incorporate positive aspirations or even lead away from them. And finally, it roots our strategy. That's why we do vision, that's how we benefit from doing it.

Okay, to continue this survey, suppose we did all that and we agreed on the economic aims that emerged. So now some questions arise: What is strategy? And how do we think about it? And how do we go about doing it?

So what is strategy?

Figuring out in broad strokes what the steps are to bring you from here to there.

Yes, strategy is a scenario that involves various aspects illuminated by the following questions: Who are the agents of change? Who are the opponents of change? What scale of agreement do we have to have before we're going to get change? What institutional structures are going to give us strength along the way?

But I want to talk at a simpler level for the moment. Forget about revolution and all the rest of that and assume you want to change a stop light in your town. How do you do it? What's the most straightforward way that you do it?

Go to the city council...

And say?

And say, "Can I have a new stop light?"

Because lack of light is leading to dogs getting killed at the intersection, or people even, whatever it is. And so you're trying to convince them of the efficacy of putting in a new light. It might work in this particular case. But suppose the city council person for some reason that you may or may not be privy to, is oblivious to your request. Maybe the city council person hates the person who makes stop lights. Whatever the reason, he isn't paying any attention to your reasonable arguments. Now what do you do?

You need to get more people together—

Why?

To show power, you know.

Well, so what's happening here? How do you win?

You're increasing the pressure.

And what happens eventually?

The pressure gets strong enough that the city council decides to give in.

The language for this straightforward idea is that you are raising the social cost of their not giving in. This city council person is attached to the no-light policy for some reason and you're creating a context in which he or she has to change behavior. If you can't appeal to reason, then you have to create a context in which you're raising social costs such that sticking to the no-light policy is more costly for the powers that be than changing the no-light policy. And it is the same for any change.

Okay, it's time to end the war in Vietnam. What are we doing if we're trying to end the war in Vietnam? It could be the Gulf War, it could be Grenada, it could be Nicaragua or Afghanistan. Pick whichever you want. It just snaps out as Vietnam for me, because that's the war for which I first learned these lessons. So what are we doing if we're trying to end a war?

Raise social costs?

Raise social costs to whom?

To those who can stop the injustice.

Okay. So how do we do that? What kinds of calculations are involved in our strategy? Suppose we have two choices. We can do a demonstration in Washington with 500,000 people and say at the demonstration, "No more war! No more war! No more war!" And we'll draw 550,000 the next time and 600,000 the next time while we're saying, "No more war! No more war!"

The other option is to bring 250,000 people saying, "No more war!" and 10,000 saying, "Smash the state!" or whatever it is they choose to say in a civil disobedience demonstration. But in any case, what they're saying is something broader and more militant than "No more war!" And they're also doing civil disobedience. And the next time maybe it'll go down to 240,000 in the big demo but up to 20,000 doing civil disobedience, and then up to 280,000 and 30,000.

Which scenario is more likely to end the war?

To answer we have to judge which scenario raises social costs higher. We'd have to know what people in position to change the policy respond to. We'd have to gauge how different options impact them. Why do we hold a demonstration in the first place? Do we think that having 500,000 people every three months in Washington always saying, "No more war! No more war!" is a cost sufficient to get them to end the war?

No, There isn't much cost for the decision makers in that.

Why isn't there much cost to that? What is it about that that doesn't seem to have any costs?

There's no increase.

That's exactly right. There's no threat, no trajectory. Of course it depends how much they care about the war. If they care about the war about as much as a chamber of commerce cares about a traffic light, they'll change it with a lot less than 500,000 people demonstrating, of course. So we might want to ask, just for the sake of being on the same terrain here, why they pursue the war. Why did they pursue the war in Vietnam, say? What's the most frequent answer given to that?

To free the bombed people?

Yes—but I am not looking for their vile answer. What's the most frequent leftist answer.

Profits.

Profits, yes. In other words to get the natural resources in Vietnam or cheap labor. But is this plausible?

No. It isn't worth that big a war for so few resources.

There's a little tiny country sitting over there. And they're going to turn into turmoil the entire U.S., redirect the entire U.S. budget and everything else for tungsten under the ground in that little country? This was not a very profound analysis on the part of the Left. It just doesn't make sense. And we could also switch to Grenada if we want to ask whether they're doing what they're doing for the resources? Nonsense. It's not for that reason. So what reason is there?

Flaunt military power?

Why would you want to flaunt power?

To show our strength and how countries should obey our dictates?

Okay, so the real issue isn't Vietnam, it's the whole empire. And what does it say if Vietnam extricates itself from our empire? What does it say if Vietnam or Nicaragua or any other country, regardless how tiny, becomes a country in which the Vietnamese or Nicaraguans or whoever else can freely utilize their own resources, energies, and capacities for their own well-being?

That others could have that outcome too.

That's called the domino effect except it's our understanding of the domino effect. The elite's presentation of the domino effect was that a cancerous entity called the Red Menace, after winning in Vietnam, would creep across the border and win as well in Thailand, from without. Our domino effect, in contrast, recognizes that if indigenous movements win in Vietnam, or Nicaragua, or even in tiny little Grenada, others might emulate their efforts elsewhere. If they can do it, with such limited means, the implication is that perhaps anybody can do it. So if they win, and they establish desirable outcomes, then there is a showcase effect. It gives tremendous energy and impetus to people elsewhere to try the same thing. So the U.S. government is not seeking tungsten but is defending the whole empire by battling up and down the Ho Chi Minh trail. And that is why they care a whole lot about their war policy, which is the point of this little exercise.

Now most people in the anti-war movement of the time didn't understand just how much they cared. They didn't understand just how serious the government was about persisting with the war—how much was at stake for the government. But, in any event, to affect war policy, to end the war, we have to raise costs. So what raises the costs? What do they care about? Go back to the conceptual tool box. It's not very full, but it'll nonetheless get us to an answer quickly. What does the side managing the war care about? Having to clean up after lots of people occupy the mall in front of the Washington Monument?

No, preserving their system.

Yes. In fact that is why they are fighting the war in the first place. In fact, it is behind pretty much everything they do. They care about preserving the positions they have in the various hierarchies and of course preserving the hierarchies themselves. The same holds true nowadays, by the way, though in a different context. So the U.S. war against Afghanistan and terrorism, most recently, is also about maintaining and enlarging domestic and international hierarchies. But the context is different. So this time the underlying logic is to respond to an attack, but to do it in a way that de-legitimates international law, that maintains national (interventionist) credibility, and that propels a new "war on terrorism." We don't go to the World Court or the UN and present evidence because to do that would legitimate such channels that could later be used by others against our policies, including our terrorism, such as for example our continuing attacks on the civilian population of Iraq, or on Afghanistan, for that matter. We rush to rain bombs on targets because that's what world powers are in business to do. It's like the mafia responding to incursions on their turf. They don't call the police. They become vigilante, even lynch mob–like, even terrorist. We are sending our familiar message to the world once again, kicked up a notch by Bush Jr.: don't obstruct our will much less strike at our interests, regardless of motivations, or you will pay an enormous price. And we propel a so-called war on terrorism, even though we are the source of most terrorism in the world—arming it, celebrating it, urging it, and in fact undertaking it—and even though such a war isn't actually a war, but instead a massacre. Because such a "war," properly conceived and pursued, can be used to induce fear in our own domestic population, and in turn to coerce it to support all manner of upward income redistribution, military spending, and draconian curbs on civil liberties that it would otherwise oppose. All this would take us way too far afield to fully pursue here, but I think it was worth noting, alongside the more familiar older example. In any event, how could we possibly raise a cost that's greater to the elite than the fear they have of losing Vietnam, or currently of losing credibility or not being able to have a war on terrorism? There's only one way.

Threaten them more than not winning the war threatens them.

Threaten the system even more. That's how far you have to go in that kind of a situation. So what does that mean? Well, how do you threaten the system even more?

Is our reasoning on target? We can actually check this with evidence for the Vietnam case. If you go back and you look at the newspapers from the Vietnam War period and examine the *Pentagon Papers*, the secret documents that that Daniel Ellsberg stole and released about Vietnam War policy making, you find something very interesting. First, if you look at the secret documents and examine their discussions of strategy you'll notice they address various policy alternatives and assess ones they want to pursue given their interests and goals. If you look at that, you discover that they'll measure a policy by its good and bad attributes. And they will never measure a war policy and say one of the bad attributes is the human travail suffered by American GIs. That doesn't show up. It's not part of their calculation any more than they would worry about the travail a tank endures. The GIs are cannon fodder. The only way they show up is whether or not you can replace one that's dead.

On the other side of the ledger, the human travail of the Vietnamese, of course, shows up as a virtue of many policies, rather than a debit. So, just so that we know whom we're dealing with, our great leaders are people who figure out the following policy: "Should we bomb military sites? Should we bomb military sites and civilian sites? Should we bomb military sites and civilian sites and use fragmentation bombs? Should we do it and use fragmentation bombs that are made out of plastic? Should we do it and use fragmentation bombs that are made out of plastic and look like toys?"

That's what they arrive at. Why? Because they drop the explosive toy, it hangs in the tree and a kid comes a long, grabs the thing, and the thing explodes and now the kid has plastic fragments throughout them. What can you not do with plastic fragments? You can't see them with x-rays. So the whole purpose of this is not to kill the kid who picks up the toy. The purpose is to destroy the infrastructure and the morale of the enemy by making the child live in a wretched state, having to be cared for by other people, as it's so hard to find and remove the plastic shrapnel. These are the kind of White House/ Pentagon minds that we're dealing with here.

Or moving back to the present, we have Afghanistan. The U.S. is attacked. There are roughly 4,000 dead. Our government decides to respond with force as the best means to maintain credibility, de-legitimate international law, and propel a new "war on terrorism" that can be used to justify diverse campaigns against international dissidents, to cajole support for enlarged military expenditures, to impose draconian assaults on liberties, and even to curb opposition to upward economic redistribution—in other words, to exploit the situation to enact policies benefiting the elite but having little or nothing to do with reducing the prospects of future terror, and even aggravating those prospects. So, how do we, the U.S., do this?

Well, we bomb them, of course, and we do it in a fashion that risks few if any U.S. casualties. Before the bombing starts and throughout its duration UN agencies and relief agencies of all sorts— Red Cross, Christian Aid, Doctors Without Borders, and many more—first warn the U.S. that bombing would create chaos throughout Afghanistan, disrupting desperate food delivery and putting as many as 7 million people at risk of starvation. And then, when the bombing starts these same groups plead with the U.S. to halt it, for the same reason. U.S. leaders do not contest the claims, nor do U.S. media and elite opinion, but instead talk positively about maintaining the assault, with no respite, through the winter. So, regardless of what in fact ultimately occurred, which as I write remains very much unknown, and will probably be forever unknown since no one is going to carefully count Afghan starvation rates, U.S. policy was perfectly willing to risk literally millions of corpses to bomb a country that was already largely rubble from decades of war, initially, ostensibly, to kill one man (who actually got away, quite predictably), and later to remove a ruling group replacing it with another that had a marginally different history—but of course really for the reasons of state mentioned above.

Opposing people who conceive these kinds of horrors is not a fun game. They don't function in a remotely civilized manner. They'll do any damn thing that they feel they need to do to achieve their ends, including things as gross as the vile examples I just described. And theirs is not a stupid calculation. I suppose you could call it a satanic logic if you wanted, but it's a natural outgrowth of where they are in our society's institutional structure, of the roles they fill and the effects of those roles on their value systems, priorities, and perceptions, and thus on how they think and act.

Okay, so that's who we're dealing with. Now if you go back to the Vietnam era, for which we have considerable evidence, and you look at their pronouncements when Congress people and prominent lawyers and doctors and corporate executives and such people decided that they were against the war, you learn something interesting. Of course these folks saw themselves as so profoundly important that they had to go on public record when they choose to go against the war. So they would hold a press conference, and they would always say the same thing, in different words, but always the same thing. They would get up and say, "I have been a strong supporter of our great courageous military's efforts in Vietnam to provide democracy and freedom to the people of Vietnam and I'm proud of that....However, in good conscience I can no longer follow this policy. I must, I am saddened to say, withdraw my support for the war in Vietnam. Our streets are in turmoil. Our next generation is being lost to us. The fabric of society is coming undone. We need to move on." These are the kinds of sentiments you see in these pronouncements. Now what are they really saying?

The costs are becoming too great.

And what's the cost? Is it that they don't like chaos?

No.

So what is it? Well, what's happening to the next generation they are talking about? The elite is perceiving and worried that the next generation is beginning to be upset not only about the war, but about the people running the war and the system molding those people. Dissenters went from saying "No more war!" to "No more system!" And not just a few fringe people did that, but it began to look like a whole new generation and many elders as well were on that path. Cries of "No more war!" became cries of "No more capitalism!" Marching became civil disobedience. Now, if you go back to the scenarios that I asked about, you can see the logic. Some people believe strategy is this unbelievably complex thing, but it isn't. These were real debates and they had real impact on the results of our efforts and thus on life and death. So this is one particular kind of calculation. And in this kind of calculation—somebody else might think otherwise and, indeed, many did, for whatever reasons—I think that those of us who were saying to demonstrate and do civil disobedience to show the progression of risk and rising cost to the elite were correct. But the main thing is to realize that it isn't just a matter of our arguing that the war is grotesque and our response has to be commensurate. It is a careful selection of actions that can win sought after gains.

Let me give you a more difficult strategic debate. Suppose you're in Boston. You're doing fantastic organizing on the campuses and developing the infrastructure of a powerful movement that could persist into the future. And you look at that and you say to yourself, "Alright, we've got something going here. We can have a lasting student movement that has student unions and very wide support and which tackles all sorts of critical matters and projects. We can link these campus resources to work in neighborhoods and workplaces and enhance that with our support." And you see that it's the quiet organizing that's making all this possible— slow and steady, sustained organizing, reaching out to new students. And you're doing all that.

But then somebody else gets up and says that while this is nice for us and for future prospects here "no one anywhere else can even see what we're doing. Nationally our work is invisible. It's great here, but it's invisible to everyone else. And as a result it doesn't do anything to help the people in Des Moines, Iowa organize against the war, or people anywhere else. What we should do is go wild in the streets, visibly. We're way ahead of everybody across the country in the number of people aroused against the war and in the level of anger attained. What we have to do is to take the consciousness and energies and resources that we already have and make ourselves visible enough so that our visible militancy prods others elsewhere into becoming active by a kind of a detonator effect."

"Now I know," the militancy advocate admits, "that when we do that, the repression and chaos here is going to make a mess of our long-term efforts, because people are going to go wild, and all the passions that are unleashed will detract from our outreach. The slow and steady organizing is going to be disrupted as a result of this choice. But on the other hand, we'll be widely visible. We won't have what we could've attained in Boston (or Berkeley or Madison) with a more patient approach, but maybe our choice will spur it to happen in St. Louis and Pittsburgh and every place else, and in any event our impact on the war will be greater."

So this was a real choice. And it came about because there could be, in this instance, a contradiction between the short-term interests of ending the Vietnam War (at least in some people's view of what could accomplish that) and the long-term interests of creating sustained movements that challenged all sorts of oppressive hierarchy. So you had to assess whether the perception was correct, and if so you had to make a choice. But our point here, now, is we can see what they were calculating. Do they build for the long haul, rather invisibly, or do they erupt for immediate impact on the social costs felt by elites in the hope that the showcase effect might inspire others to do likewise? There is no universal answer. It depends on context, on what acts will have what effects, and on what benefits can come from sustained efforts.

Rather than spend too much time on the details of that example, I would like to go on to another broad, but very related, set of issues if we can.

What's a reform?

It's a change that doesn't fundamentally alter the system.

Okay, a reform is a change that is consistent with the main defining features of the system. What's ending the war in Vietnam? Or in Afghanistan?

No one wants to answer—well, it's a reform. There's no way that ending the war in Vietnam is in-and-of itself changing fundamental institutions. And it's the same for any war. Ending the war in Vietnam, any war, is a decree. The war is over. It's not a change in institutional structure.

What's winning a strike and getting higher pay?

A reform.

Yes. Most gains that we might win are reforms. In fact, everything is a reform except fundamentally changing role structures that are critical to hierarchies that define society's center and boundary in its four spheres. That's not reform, because that's revolution. Now is there something bad about reforms—you reformist, you?

Reformists don't go for the total picture.

Well, the war was ended.

But you said that's just a reform. That's not a change.

Reform doesn't equal lack of change. There can be change short of revolution. Moreover, there aren't two things—revolution and change—that seek to stabilize existing relations, which is probably more the distinction you really have in mind.

Let's think about this some more because this problem befuddles many activists. Is the right way to formulate this issue as though we have only these two options? Do we want to have concepts regarding this facet of what we care about that distinguish only system-reproducing change on the one hand, and revolution on the other hand? Can we only be either for reforms of the first sort or for revolution? Can we fight only for reforms that maintain the systemic status quo or for revolution? Does this demarcation of reality, which is quite typical among many leftists, make sense?

I think it makes no sense whatever, posed this way, though a lot of people think they are being quite informed and astute when they suggest you are either for reform or you are for revolution.

Reforms are completely necessary, sure, but often the reforms are used to placate those that actually want revolution.

Okay, that certainly happens. But unless you think that there is a scenario in which the world becomes wonderful overnight, with no smaller steps in the process, reforms matter. In the overnight scenario, reforms are a waste of time. Let's work toward the evening on which the transformation happens and not waste our time on anything less. But any realistic scenario involves a sequence of steps involving a lot of struggle. Calling somebody a reformist pejoratively simply because they want to win reforms makes no sense. In the real world where things don't happen so quickly, no matter how revolutionary you are you should be for reforms because they are the building blocks of change. This is something that young people tend to sometimes get lost on because of the also correct insight that reforms are not necessarily intrinsically system challenging. So seeing this latter fact, you become critical of reform and you start to feel that anything that involves a reform must be a sell-out. But is that sensible?

Let's come at this slightly differently. What's a good reform? Being strategic about it, what do we want to have for the characteristics of a reform we will be happy to win? To foreshadow next chapter, we want to make people's lives better, of course. But there's another thing that we'd like to have be the result of a reform victory. We want a change such that we are left in a position to win still more gains. Optimally, we're winning the possibility or the likelihood of being able to win still more. That's not a small insight and we'll take it further next chapter.

9. Reform and Revolution

There is a time when the operation of the machine becomes so odious, makes you so SICK AT HEART, that you can't take part; and you've got to put your bodies upon the gears and upon the wheels, upon the levers, upon all the apparatus and you've got to make it stop.

—Mario Savio

Works are of value only if they give rise to better ones.

—Von Humboldt

Jesse Jackson is working to build the Rainbow Coalition (or Ralph Nader is working to build the Green Party), as a means to win power in the U.S. He passes through New Hampshire. What should be his standards for evaluating what he's doing? In other words, what is a victory when he comes out the other side of New Hampshire? What should he be trying to accomplish?

Organize people. Leave something behind. Leave behind people who have a movement of their own and heightened consciousness.

And what's the other possible set of standards?

Get votes.

One set of standards could be to get votes. So if you go in and you have 2% and you come out and you have 8%, that's a fantastic success. But there's another set of standards which is that you go in and there's some level of grassroots organization present and some level of consciousness present, and when you come out, there's more. This is a large difference in outlook. It is easy to express, there's nothing complicated about it, and yet it is a hugely important difference, especially once we elaborate it into a more general set of norms.

You're organizing an anti-war demonstration. You're about to organize. You want to bring as many people as you can to your event. Why? To raise the social cost. You want people to be as aroused and militant as they can be. So, you go out and you give speeches and interact with folks and you begin to develop demands, as well. And you come up with a clever slogan about going to Washington to shut down the city and ending the war by your demonstration called for Mayday. And the idea is you bring people to Washington to do civil disobedience throughout the city, jamming the streets, and you close down the government, and you end the war. So, when you give speeches about this, you could talk in a sober, informative, compelling fashion to convey what you have in mind. Or you could talk in a highly emotional impassioned way about shutting down the government and ending the war on Mayday. Which choice do you make? These are strategic choices. Do you use the slogan "If the government won't stop the war we'll stop the government. We're coming to Washington to stop the government and thereby stop the war"? Is there any problem with it?

It seems like it might be upsetting, depressing, if you do get a bunch of people and you do block a lot of the streets, and the war doesn't end.

Exactly. But imagine trying to argue this as you just have—that the slogan and especially the surrounding rhetoric in proposed speeches and literature is misleading—to a big meeting of 400 very excited and aroused people planning this event. They're all screaming, "Stop the government! Stop the war!" and getting off on it. Mayday is the end of the horror. You are going to have a hard time sobering things up. One side is saying, "We need this catchy slogan and logic. We need to arouse passions and energies by talking about ending the war at this event. The other side is saying, we can be emotional about the human travail of war, but about what we are doing we have to be very clear. We are raising the social cost, and doing it a bit at a time. It is a long process. We are not ending the war in a day, and we need people to understand that if they are going to stay with this project for the long haul."

You can see that that may be a difficult message to convey unless people already have a developed sense of how to think about these type issues. But it is the right message, I think; just think of the alternative. What happens if people go and disrupt and then the war doesn't end?

Misery.

How succinct. If you are involved in trying to win social change and your perceptions and standards for what achieving gains means are never fulfilled, you may get depressed. If your standards for success can't be met, it is a prescription for constantly feeling defeated. You always think you've lost. It's infinitely harder to keep involved because what you are doing seems doomed. If you have false standards, if you don't even know what success is, if the main organizers misunderstand the war and think, "Oh, it's just a bad policy. If we go down there and mess up the streets of Washington, they're going to turn off the war and we're going to have beaten them," then you will feel your actions have failed when the results don't meet the rhetoric. If you think that way or if you manipulatively use that kind of rhetoric to try to get people to come to the event (because, after all, who wouldn't give up a Sunday morning to end the war) you are undercutting the logic of your own movement. If people demonstrate and go home and saying, "We were there. We stopped the city. And we did not stop the war," they will be frustrated rather than empowered.

What's the alternative?

Our mindset should be we're going to Washington to raise consciousness and if as a result we raise a little consciousness and we have a few more people involved and we have some more alliances and a little more infrastructure, that's a big success. And the difference in these two approaches to the same event—and now it ought to be obvious that it could be about Vietnam, or nuclear power, or racism, or globalization, or anything on the social agenda—is a big part of the difference between those who stick to the process for the long haul and those who join but then just as quickly quit. Knowing what you are doing, you can see achievements, and you stay engaged because you are accomplishing something. But if you only hear inflated rhetoric and are recruited on the basis of false expectations, you may get frustrated. Those who know what's going on will feel like their efforts have great merit. But those who don't understand the sequential logic of dissent will feel like their efforts were worthless, and many of them will quit, and then activists have to get more people to replace the ones that become disenchanted, just to not lose ground.

You notice in this discussion, there's not much theory. Our conceptual framework can help us figure out what demands make sense, what constituencies ought to be organized, what issues are central and connected with our aims, and what focuses we ought to incorporate. It can help us generate vision to produce hope, inspiration, and orientation, as well. But analyzing specific tactical choices almost always rests mostly on our understanding of people, of feelings, of shared viewpoints. It is more direct, more experiential, and more rooted in past life lessons.

I'm just wondering about—it's very hard to measure reform. I think that's one of the problems with it for me, and for other people who think like me. I mean, you see some reforms and it's not *clear if what's called a reform is really even a reform. Take a union working to get an increase in wages, a $.75 increase. They're holding out. Finally, the international notices. They get rid of a couple of the more radical labor leaders and then they settle on a $.30 increase at a five-year contract. Now on one level they've managed to take some more wages that capitalists and workers struggle over. On the other hand, they've disempowered the people who were engaged in the struggle in the first place and have perhaps reduced the possibility of what could've happened afterwards if they had actually held out and achieved more of what they were seeking. So, I guess it's very hard for me to evaluate what constitutes reform.*

Right on schedule. We are back on track for this chapter: reform or revolution. Thank you.

Well, first they're all reforms. If people win changes short of redefining structures, they have won reforms. But you want to distinguish among reforms, and I agree with you. I also want to. So how about if we create a new concept. That's what we do when our conceptual tool box isn't adequate: we expand it. Let's call this new thing we want to pay close attention to a non-reformist reform. This is a new concept, a name for something that exists and that we want to pay attention to. It refers to something in the world that we care about. It draws a new border, highlights another reality, and focuses us in a new way. Remember that's why we create concepts. That's what radical theory is all about. And a non-reformist reform is a strategy-related concept that's designed precisely to be part of a broader trajectory leading to fundamental change, that has as its criteria of success not only winning some particular policies and demands, but also creating the conditions from which more gains might be won in the future. So that's a non-reformist reform, while, in contrast, a reformist reform is one that's an end unto itself.

I think this is a useful distinction. It's a useful way of thinking that makes it crystal clear that one can fight for things short of revolution that are still part of a process that leads to revolutionary change. Reforms can be part of a process that wins more and more gains as time goes along, or reforms can lead to a dead end—or they can fall between, as well. I think this concept is a tool for coping with the problem that you're talking about so that in each case you have to ask whether some particular struggle is for a non-reformist reform or merely a reformist reform, and to what degree and with what qualities.

Take anything you want to address, any of the real and serious issues that activists debate about. You can usefully analyze choices and issues in terms of the concepts we are developing. Is a proposed demand or project a non-reformist reform or a reformist reform? This is determined partly by attributes of the end you are seeking, but largely by how you are seeking those ends, by the steps you are taking, by what you are teaching. Does your approach raise conscious in the constituencies that need to be affected? Does it have the positive impact on organizational structure one wants to have? Does it raise social costs that can win new gains that empower prospects for still further gains? Is it part of the process of going from one side of the bridge to the other side, from where we are to our goals?

So in the case of the union battle that you mention, one side is thinking strategically, namely the management side. And the other side is often not thinking strategically, namely our side, the workers' side. Workers are looking for a particular achievement, $.75 more per hour or some such thing. And when you see the type result you describe, a partial victory, what it often indicates is that the management combatant has said, "Alright, we'll give up part of what they are seeking on this particular issue, because that is the way conditions are pushing us, but we are very concerned about not providing our adversaries a stage they can use to advance further from." So they combine the slight wage increase with other changes that seek to disempower the union. And you think, "Wait, did we really win, or did we only appear to win and actually lose?"

I'll give you a really stark example of that. Take the Vietnam War again. Suppose you're the government. Now be strategic from their point of view, not from our point of view. First of all, what are they worried about in the war in Vietnam? What are they most worried about?

The domino effect.

The domino effect. The real domino effect, that is, that the Vietnamese will extricate themselves from colonial and neo-colonial subservience and establish a kind of showcase that inspires others to do likewise. So if they begin to realize that they're going to have to leave Vietnam without actually winning the war itself, what is it important for them to do?

Destroy the domino?

This isn't very difficult is it. You could get a job with the Pentagon in a flash. So they engage in actions that make some things clear to everyone watching: "Okay, maybe you can win a military battle against us in some technical sense of that word if you persevere long and hard enough, if you will take enough casualties, if you can get enough international support, and also support inside the U.S. population. Maybe you can get out from under our boot to some extent, but when you do get out from under the boot, you're going to be living on the moon. There will be nothing left."

So the last bombings in the war of course are the worst bombings of the war. And not only that, in addition to all the other things we do, we go in there and we try and inflame every racial passion that we can. We divide and conquer. We literally do that inside Vietnam and Laos and Cambodia, so that all that will be left after the dust clears is hostility and destruction. We even plant the goddamn bombs under the ground so they'll be blowing up for thirty years. We, the U.S. that is, lose a part of the battle but we transform the stage so that we have in fact won the war by preventing the domino dynamic and preventing a showcase effect of a viable extrication from our empire.

Or take the case of Cuba. The U.S. messes up its strategy by insufficiently supporting Batista. Led by Fidel Castro and Che Guevara the Cubans battle out from under, structurally. So now what? If we look at terrorism in the case of Cuba and the world, and we create a little pile of all the terrorist acts all over the world except those directed at Cuba and then we create a pile of the terrorist acts during the same period of time (from the Cuban revolution to now) that were directed at Cuba, I don't know which stack is bigger, but we'll notice that they're pretty close. Now why is that? Because, the Cubans managed, due to a variety of factors, to get out from under our boot. They didn't do exactly what I would like to see people do, but that was because I think in their particular case, they couldn't. They didn't have the means. As the U.S., we can't let an emerging society get too good, too worthy of emulation. So we have to bomb them in any conflict, and terrorize and isolate them afterward.

Showcase effects are potentially disastrous. We aren't worried the Cubans are going to send some folks to Guatemala much less Kansas. We are very worried the Guatemalans are going to look at Cuba and say, "Hell, we can do that too!" and they will welcome the few Cubans who come to Guatemala. We're worried that even without the Cuban visitors they will start to struggle for themselves with great hope, passion, and confidence, inspired by the Cuban showcase. So we do all kinds of things to try and make Cuba a less pleasant sight.

Or take a labor-related issue even larger than the one you raised. If unions are established as a right, if the labor movement wins the right to have unions, does capital say, "Okay, screw it, we lost"? No. There is now a new terrain. Now workers will have unions, true, but the capitalists will therefore switch gears from trying to prevent unions from existing at all, to doing the best they can to get unions to be less effective, to tie them up in legal constraints, and so on and so forth.

From all this it follows that if we activists are as serious about attaining liberation as the elite are about defending hierarchy, we have to be at least as strategic as they are, though with our very different aims.

But now we encounter a new problem. Some people on the Left don't like being strategic. They think being strategic corrupts us. They want us to play nice and be gentle. What they want is something like a kind of basketball game we made up and used to play back in the Sixties. In this game you aren't concerned with winning, but with the quality of play. You play to make everyone else play better and have a good time, even your opponents. You pass the ball not to win, but to raise the quality of the experience and the pleasure of all involved. You play hard, but not with an eye on the score. If you are much better than the person you are defending is, you try to interact with her or him to get the best joint result. You don't just steal the ball over and over with your far greater speed and skills. If you are much better than the person defending you, you don't keep scoring on them easily; you scale back and interact, again, so the dance between you is at the highest level of joint skill as you can elicit. So clearly if we're playing this type of basketball against capitalists, they are going to annihilate us. Because they not only play with their eyes on the basket, but also they own the referees and will foul us to death. And all too often, this is what we're doing, it seems to me. We're not making coherent arguments about our aims and our methods, and we are not taking seriously just how vile our opponents are, and we are not doing what needs to be done to win, and to win again, and again.

If you have ever played chess this same point may become clear by thinking about how you play. Most folks play it reflexively. There is no plan at work, just an almost spontaneous reaction to each new move. We move knee-jerk-this and knee- jerk-that, immediate-reaction-this and immediate-reaction-that, this move feels good and that move feels good. But the moves are not part of a plan, and we lose. It isn't so easy, in fact, to discipline oneself to think carefully about each move, in context of all others, in terms of available options, with a plan. A real plan is a comprehension of who must become our allies, what kind of organizations we need to create, what kinds of methods we need to use, and what winning sequence of non-reformist reforms we should undertake in light of our needs, capacities, and aims.

What scale of support do you think we need to win in the United States?

Massive.

Massive meaning?

Wide scale throughout the country. Huge numbers of people. Way more than the majority.

Well, you may be right, but I think it's actually a lot less than that, probably about a third of folks activist oriented, maybe even somewhat less.

It's an interesting question because obviously it has a lot to do with what we have to do now, to prepare for winning later. As you are getting close to winning, what is it that you've accomplished? 98% of the country on your side and active? Or do you have something much less, but sufficient? Well, if you don't have any notion about that—and clearly our views change as we learn more—then we have little idea of what we need to be doing in the present. I would say we need something like a third on our side actively believing in struggle for change; and about a third will be watching TV and on the sidelines, waiting to see what happens, leaning this way or that way rather weakly; and then there may also be about a third on the other side, but the third on the other side are mostly on the other side weakly.

But what about the army?

Well, what about the army? Are we ever going to beat the U.S. army in a violent struggle?

No.

That's right. It is uncontestable. Totally obvious. So I have to wonder why so many people on the Left have such a hard time with this issue. What can we deduce has to happen? If the quick answer is that we're not going to beat them in a violent scrimmage, what's the alternative?

You can't win.

Well, that's one answer, and I think deep down it's probably what most people, even on the Left, believe—which is a very serious problem for us. But there is another answer...

You subvert it.

Yes, the point is, if we have a big movement and we've got one third really active but they've got the whole damn army and the police force and everything else armed against us, then we can't win. It's impossible.

But if we've got a third active, what does that mean in terms of the army? Well, the army is still under the control of the government but at various times the army has in a lot of places refused to fire upon their own people. And not only because they were infiltrated—there would have to be some consciousness there—but there'd also have to be links.

Links to families and other working people...

Exactly. If there's an uprising in Watts in Los Angeles, do they call the National Guard unit that lives in the neighborhood to put down the disturbance? No, if possible they call the paratroopers that are in some state far away and they'll often try to find a state that has a community that will feel most hostile to the area where the strife is, and they'll bring them in. So they know what they're doing. They don't want to ask the army to do things that will challenge people's loyalty and lead to resistance. But we don't wait for the army to spontaneously fall apart, we make it fall apart. So that's part of a strategy. That's in fact when you're really getting somewhere. And we were really getting somewhere at one time. The most courageous organizing in many ways around the war in Vietnam was by those people who said, "Okay, I'm against the war—where do I sign up? I'm against the war—let me in. Because I'm going in there and I'm going to organize opposition inside the military." So there was growing broad dissent, and growing dissolution of repressive structures, as well.

But for the person who goes into the army as an organizer, it's very difficult to do. And there were even some people who joined the police force with the same thing in mind in that period. In Chicago there were people who did that. That's very serious. Well, everything worthy is serious, but you can see how that's an important part of the process. And you can see how these choices can be components of a strategy. But whatever it is that you're doing, from trying to win a new traffic light to trying to stop a war, to winning council democracy in your neighborhood and in your factory, or whatever it is you're trying to do, it's the same kind of calculations you're making. Sometimes they're difficult moral calculations. Sometimes they're just hard calculations because we really don't know enough to judge options confidently. But always we're trying to string together actions and structures that lead from where we are to where we want to wind up.

If there're a lot of reforms, we get some little changes but the system is still there and it'll just find different ways to get you back to where you were.

That's what our theory tells us, yes. Our current understanding is that the four spheres have institutions that mold outcomes consistently with the reproduction of their role structures. We need to enlarge the viewpoint, refine it, but that's what it suggests. However, society isn't seamless. It isn't perfect. Its rules of motion aren't like the laws of gravity. We can intervene. Indeed, that is the whole point of our projects.

Suppose we say that we want to win liberation and we have some set of visions. And our vision is a serious, well-conceived, liberatory goal. So it's not going to be attained tomorrow. It's going to take a long time. Maybe it's going to take twenty-five or fifty years. Maybe it's going to take one hundred years. We don't know how long. But the process of winning is obviously going to include a lot of dimensions. First of all, there're fifty human years there. So alleviating pain during that period is not just a strategic thing. It's not just tactical. If you're a human being who cares about other human beings, you'd better care about how much pain and how much pleasure people are experiencing over those fifty years, and not just after you win. Indeed, if your way of viewing the world is such that it makes you cold to alleviating those immediate pains, forget it. You're not going to organize anybody. No one will pay you any heed.

But it isn't the case that reforms, that is efforts on people's parts to improve life in the present, have to reproduce current defining relations. They can begin to subvert them. They can lead toward new structures and larger more empowered movements. They can eventually win defining changes. That's what the anti-apartheid movement did. It's what the anti-slavery movement achieved. These were not only important gains in people's lives at that time, they were fundamental changes in underlying institutions.

What about the idea that the worse it is the better the prospects are?

Well, it is sometimes true that a horrible event or process can unleash forces for change. But that hardly makes a case for advocating horrible events or processes. That's a crazy viewpoint. And it obviously wouldn't endear an organizer to those people who endure the worst suffering, were the organizer to propose aggravating their suffering further. With that attitude we would be as much an enemy as the government is.

But it's also strategically wrong in other senses. Yes, sometimes worse contexts may encourage increased radicalism. If the cops go wild and swing their clubs unexpectedly, all of a sudden people might have an enlightening experience and some of them might last as revolutionaries for thirty years. But it's just as likely that in horrible times folks will only seek to return to prior better times rather than seeking a radical transformation to go forward. They may just want to eliminate the worst evils, in tune with returning to past conditions that weren't quite so bad. That is a more typical response to economic woes, in fact. It sees calamities as deviations from progress, not spurs to progress. More, you can't usefully have a movement mindset that encourages visiting pain on people. That won't sustain a worthwhile movement.

Take for instance, the Seattle Liberation Front circa 1969 or so. (We can avoid current controversy and think about this without personal stakes in the discussion. The lessons are applicable in the present, however.) It was a group of people. These were mostly men from elite schools, Cornell, mostly, and a bunch of other schools, I think. Some of them are still around in the Left. Not very many, I bet. And these folks decided, "Okay, let's go to Seattle and let's help the revolution." Of course, one problem with their desire was that as people who lacked a good conceptual tool box they thought they were going to win in twenty minutes. They were going to help make the revolution overnight. Now they didn't have any serious notion of what they wanted for a new society. They just figured, "Okay, we're on our side of the bridge to the future. We want to get to the other side of the bridge. If you've got people jumping up and down, they're moving. Once they are moving, they'll move in a good direction. So, let's create chaos. Create turmoil. Create dissidence. Create repression. Make things worse to get things better. Folks will move. They will go over the bridge. Hooray! Revolution!"

So they went into Seattle with this fantastic conception and just provoked wild activity in the town for a little while. Literally, they sought to produce bedlam. And about three or four months later, I don't remember exactly how long (maybe it was six months later, maybe less, whatever) the radical women of Seattle ran them out of town. The dynamics created by this group were so sexist and so macho and so insensitive to people's lives and circumstances in all manner of ways that their actions were totally destructive of left possibilities. And the women's movement basically told them good-bye. So that's an example of people operating with no vision and no strategy, or perhaps one might say a very simple strategy. Their view was just that motion works.

But sometimes a change isn't even good, ultimately. Sometimes it just defuses us and wins little or nothing...

Co-optation, we can call that. Yes, it happens that sometimes a movement accepts way less than it is in position to win, or even worse, accepts some status or income for its leaders and nothing for the constituencies it was meant to serve. But that is just vile, and even if one is reformist in the sense of fighting only for the immediate gain, with no longer-term goal in place, that is still vile.

What about ecology? It seems a horribly compromised movement to me.

Ecology wasn't a sphere in our conceptual picture. It's because fish aren't a constituency group that is a self-conscious actor in society. So even though ecology is profoundly important and has huge impact, there is no group creating a set of aims and agendas due to the specific position it occupies with respect to ecology. So you can imagine a set of policies around the ecology that represents the interests of any group that we can talk about. You can imagine a sexist or anti-sexist set of policies around the ecology, one that embodies patriarchal or non-patriarchal values. And capitalists can in fact be seriously concerned about ecological problems because the problems affect them too. So they can be concerned, that is, about whether or not there are seals to look at in their harbor but not give a damn about whether or not toxic waste is being dumped miles away on some Black community.

I think the ecology organizations that are having the detrimental effect you noted, you will find if you investigate, have horrible class politics. If movement life involved just one axis to struggle around, and all you had to do is worry about that one axis, you'd always know who your friend is and who your enemy is. It would all be crystal clear, with maybe an occasional minor complication. But with four primary axes of influence and change, plus ecology and international relations, the same people can be seeking good and bad outcomes simultaneously, regarding two different domains—and so can movements. So we have to deal with these complications and being able to coherently see the relationships and talk about them is very advantageous.

There's no general answer other than to go in and think about possibilities and analyze them and try and figure them out. I have concerns, like you, with ecology movements for these reasons. I think it's the easiest irritation, so to speak, to co-opt and it's the easiest one to get sidetracked. On the other hand, it's very powerful because it can unite so many different constituencies. And thus you find that the Greens perhaps come closest to the kind of perspective that we've been trying to elaborate in our concept-building project. The Greens are the activist group that seems closest to the multi-focused approach we are advocating. But they are also movements for ecological this and ecological that which I don't want to be in the same room with. They're more concerned about whether or not they're going to be able walk across the beach without seeing a dead bird than they are about whether some worker is going to lose her job or work in a toxic environment.

Or take the very powerful anti-nuke movement of the Eighties, where we can again look to the past to avoid current, immediate controversies, but benefit from the lessons from the past that are relevant now and into the future. What did No Nukes mean? First of all, if you didn't want nukes for electricity, then you had to want or at last be willing to put up with something else. And in the real world what is that something else? Well you may have wanted solar or wind or something, but in reality, at the time, less nuclear meant you were advocating maintaining or enlarging coal mining.

Fossil fuels.

Exactly. That was the operative choice at the time. So suppose all you said was "No Nukes! No Nukes! No Nukes! Nukes hurt people. No Nukes! Nukes are a chainsaw cutting butter. No Nukes!" And you never mentioned coal mines. What would that tell those who are listening to you about your view of the world? How about looking at coal mines to see what coal mining does to human beings? It never comes up. Now I'm not saying anti-nuke is the wrong position. But do you see how narrow it is when the position is arrived at without attention to the impact coal has? If all anti-nuke activists are thinking about is effects on people and society, why aren't they also concerned about what the alternative is?

It seems to be an intrinsic problem with groups that define themselves in terms of opposition.

Well, I think being defined in terms of opposition rather than positive goals is certainly part of the problem, and so is defining movements in terms of one dimension of life and not all of them. Those approaches are a problem. Reactive politics is ultimately self-defeating. If all we're ever doing is reacting, we're never seeking anything positive. And that's not going to attract many people. But returning to this No Nukes example, it really is of consequence when you look and you see the effects of mining on coal miners compared with the effects of a nuclear power plant on the community. Which is worse?

Coal mining. But what about solar and wind power?

But that wasn't a real option. Of course that's the better choice, if and when you can win it on a scale to really replace nukes and/or coal. But in the short run, people were trying to shut down reactors so the real choice was to close nuclear and use more coal, or maintain or expand nuclear and use less coal. Okay, solar is better, to the extent you can employ it, obviously. And so you want a movement that whatever else it's saying about these short-term options, is saying something compelling about using good approaches in the long run, assuming it's possible. But I don't want to debate solar now. We'd have to investigate it, figure it out, etc. But versus the coal mine, it is pretty clear that the coal mine is doing a whole lot more damage to human beings than nukes, isn't it?

It's not clear.

Why?

It depends on the nuclear power and whether or not something goes wrong.

Exactly. If nothing major goes wrong, there really is no comparison. Coal is infinitely worse for the people doing the work. So, a reasonable person could come out against nuclear power saying basically that the risk is just too great. Right now nuclear power is pretty good, actually, in that it isn't hurting people near as much as coal mining hurts people. But if nuclear goes bad once every fifty years, the one time it goes bad, what will that mean? Well, it might be interesting to see how many people die in coal mines and from accumulated diseases due to working in mines in fifty years and how many people get black lung and everything else.

Not just that. You're also talking about the effect of nuclear waste over thousands of years.

Yes, and so you have to take that into account. But do you see that it is one thing to list all the nuke problems and compare them with coal problems, properly accounted, and then say, "No Nukes!" and it is quite another thing to list them and ignore the ills of coal mining. The second option doesn't even recognize the plight of the miners. They simply don't count. They are not part of the perception.

So, I too was for No Nukes, in fact, but I didn't get along too well with a lot of people that were for No Nukes. And that's because their opposition was oblivious to class issues. And that's also why the No Nukes movement was weaker than it could've been. It's because a lot of people didn't get along well with No Nukes advocates and had good reason to not get along with them. It's because the No Nukes movement was very classist. It was a movement that didn't express itself very well to working people, not because it was a stupid movement that didn't know how to talk clearly, but because it just didn't care much about working people or, at least, it didn't think about working people's issues clearly and didn't really understand them.

So the lesson is that we need a conceptual framework that doesn't allow that kind of narrow-minded movement to develop, as the concepts in the framework would either prevent us from being so blind to centrally important aspects of life, or at least clarify about those who are so blind that they are not worthy of support.

What we are developing may not be such a conception. But you can see that in the world where we operate, we need a framework that pushes against our having critical blind spots in our perceptions and valuations. It is just a fact of life, especially given socialization methods and schooling, that the odds are that potential leftists are going to have to have relative blind spots, with one kind of bias or another, depending on who we are. We're not super people. We're not saints.

Everybody's going to have a tendency to be less attuned to some facets of life and more attuned to others due to our experiences and feelings. Everybody is pushed by circumstances and experiences, which are often relatively narrow. So it helps if we have a framework that continually pushes against these kinds of bias, which is therefore one of the things we should think about when we're not only creating theory and figuring out vision, but especially when we're figuring out strategy.

10. Strategic Options

The validity of a particular theory is a matter of its logical derivation from the general assumptions which it makes. But its applicability to a given situation depends upon the extent to which its concepts actually reflect the forces operating in that situation.

–Lionel Robbins

Woe betide those who seek to save themselves the pain of mental building by inhabiting dead men's minds.

–G.D.H. Cole

Let's continue by addressing a few more examples of broad strategic issues. Let's start this time with a question: What is criticism/self-criticism?

Analysis.

Well, what does it mean?

Self-criticism is like a model used in Maoist brochures. This is how I understand it. An activist would criticize something the group was doing, or criticize themselves for their feelings and the group would respond, and people would criticize them and it was this mutual criticism process that was supposed to elevate their politics.

Yes, that is precisely right. It was meant to uncover false ideas and behaviors and to correct them, which seems like a nice idea. You have a tactical tool to improve your actions. A strategy is really a scenario that involves a sequence of tactics such as strikes, demonstrations, civil disobedience, criticism/self-criticism, walks, marches. These are all tactical things that you can piece together into a campaign. And you can piece a lot of campaigns into a scenario. So do we put this or that tactic in our tactical tool box or not? Criticism/self-criticism: yes or no? It's a serious question.

It seemed like an okay idea to lots of people in the U.S. Left, for example, thirty years ago, but it might be that Americans, because of who we are and our culture and everything else about us, will take criticism/self-criticism and in twenty-nine minutes transform it into tear my head off/tear his head off. So it might not be a good idea because beautiful desires aside, it might not work properly in our milieu, given who our institutional boundary has made us.

But because the Chinese did it, and after all, their movement won, we did it too, but unwisely—because we wanted to wear the same suspenders that Trotsky wore, or the same hat that Mao wore, more or less. I am serious about this. That's what people in various sects do. They emulate some hero mindlessly, I believe, even down to clothing, often. In fact, I can go around the U.S. right now and if I run into somebody who was a Weatherman, even someone who hasn't been political in thirty years, I bet there's a good chance that I will recognize some of the intonations in their voice patterns. In these groups, the dominant personality's attributes tend to spread through the whole group. So after a time they all talk alike. They walk alike. They share mannerisms and choice of clothing. They wear the same stuff—usually outfits that make them look like Lenin or whoever it is they want to look like. Anyway, these are seemingly strange points to raise, but in fact they're real problems and issues that people can be sensitized to and that we can do a lot better regarding. This is not just trivia, in fact.

So the idea of criticism/self-criticism, to return to that particular tactic, is consequential. You keep trying to do it, trying to do it, trying to do it, because true revolutionaries do it. But for us it is self-defeating nonsense, because at least as it is formulated, it doesn't work here. It doesn't lead to good results here. So we have to come up with some other method to accomplish the sought ends—finding weaknesses and correcting them—which are certainly important to achieve. We have to ask, "What's the goal of that technique?" And if that goal is worthwhile, fine, we need a technique to accomplish it, but we may need a different technique to accomplish it than was used elsewhere. How can we do the useful thing given who we are and where we are? So we seek the goal, if we decide it is worthy, but we don't use a method that doesn't work.

Here's another example of a kind of operational dynamic or symptom the Left often has that we need to guard against. Tom Hayden was a leftist who is still progressive but is different now than he was then—but in any event he's a very smart guy and he's got some considerable insights. And one of his insights is that leftists have a tendency to snatch defeat from the jaws of victory. What does he mean by that? And why does it happen?

When we win something, who's going to be the one who delivers it? Will we deliver it? Will we get up on TV and say, "Yesterday we won an end to the war. Hooray for us"? No. So, who will do it? The state will do it. And what does the state get up and say? Can you imagine Lyndon Johnson or Richard Nixon or Bill Clinton or George Bush coming on and saying, "Due to the courageous activities of the anti-war movement, it has been revealed that I am a slimy bastard warmonger who's trying to enrich the rich and impoverish the poor and annihilate Vietnam/Afghanistan and, therefore—"? No you can't imagine that. But you can imagine them having been forced by movements to relent and then saying that despite the stupid lunatics in the street who have tied our hands for so long in our efforts to reach a just conclusion of this war, we have finally reached the just conclusion the slimy lunatics have demanded.

And the leftist watching this listens and actually snatches defeat from the jaws of victory because she believes what she is hearing, or is horrified and demeaned by it. Leftists get upset when it turns out that the person who signs the decree for the thing the movement fought for doesn't give the movement credit for the accomplishment.

Well, what did we expect? If we understand what's going on, that shouldn't unduly depress us because it is entirely predictable. But these are real processes that happen; this one happens due to ignorance on our part. These are not little dynamics. These are the kinds of phenomena that can slowly but surely rip movements to shreds. Slowly but surely they can disillusion or depress activists. Regrettably, there are many things that can do that. We have to get a grip on all of them, and that's another thing our concepts are for, if we use them well.

To take still another example, what about the phrase "the personal is political"? What does that mean?

It's like...you wouldn't be able to apply some sort of macro-political vision if you don't live it yourself on the personal level.

That's what it has come to mean—for some people, anyhow. It's a kind of a hypocrisy argument. But it also could mean, and this was in fact its original meaning, that personal acts are often political by their logic and implications and more particularly, in their causes. And what the insight was supposed to do was to sensitize people to paying attention to the stuff that is called personal from a political angle. It was supposed to attune us to the fact that personal depression, personal poverty, and seemingly personal inadequacies usually aren't personal failings at all, but are, instead, the product of social forces. The focus was on the daily indignities of sexism, suffering an abusive husband, suffering household confinement, the indignities of race and of class, the poverty and the depression, the self destructive choices, the personal hardship—and the message was that all this is social, not personal. Yes, it afflicts us personally, but its roots are in social relations. The effects are shared, not private. The solutions are political, not individual.

But now consider the hypocrisy interpretation. What's the extreme version of it? The extreme version is that each person's every act is political and this is what it means to be political—to oversee your personal choices and make them wonderful. So you sit around and you figure out what the absolute perfect human being is. What he eats. What she wears. What he watches. What she reads. And now any deviation from being that perfect human being is failure and in the worst case such a deviation makes a person a slimeball. The person who falls short in their personal choices is not practicing the right politics because their lifestyle deviates from perfect. We go from the personal is political as an insight that large-scale political phenomena impact our personal lives and are at the root of many pains that seem entirely personal to us, to nearly the opposite mentality. That is, in the new reading everything is entirely personal and it is our narrow, individual personal choices that constitute all that is politics.

I don't know enough about the rest of the world to know whether this is a largely American problem, or whether this is a characteristic of the particular conjuncture of capitalism and everything else that we have in this society, or what. But we definitely have an all or nothing mentality, especially young people. So it leads to this kind of attitude where correct insights (that what we do has political implications) are pushed down a slippery slope until they become impossibly extreme (that the only thing that matters politically are our private personal daily life choices, our lifestyles).

In fact, the idea that one is going to be perfect overnight is horribly self defeating, even if we knew what perfect personal choices were—indeed even if such a thing actually existed. People who think their political focus should be attaining some kind of perfect lifestyle generally have a very short tenure in political life. They last maybe two years, maybe four years of political life. During that time, they're never perfect. They set standards for themselves that they're not going to meet. They set standards for others that others won't meet. They berate themselves and each other, endlessly. And it just doesn't work. There's no sense of patience. There's no sense of humanity and mutual respect and modesty in it. They just become these lifestyle norms that destroy rather than enhance humanity, and in any event have little to do with political effectiveness.

What I am saying doesn't mean that we shouldn't pay attention to our behavior. We should, of course. But honestly paying attention to behavior is different than what these folks do. Because if we're honestly paying attention to our behavior it would include being sensitive to the fact that people take some time to develop good traits and habits and that what is good for one person may not be good for another. That would reflect sensitivity.

Here's another example of the decisions that face us: What about violence? Or what about Leninist organization called democratic centralism?

Those too raise real issues that involve clear choices. Now violence and democratic centralism are both like criticism/self-criticism in the sense that they're tactics. We could use either of these, or we could use one, or we could use neither. Are violence and democratic centralism in our tool box, or should we throw either or both out because they are counter-productive, that's the question. Are Leninist organization and violence tactics that we can use in the course of the campaigns, struggles, and scenarios we seek? Or is there something about them that's just so horrible that we can't even conceivably use them?

Are you using those as two different things or are you saying violence—

Yes, they are two different things. Okay, we can do either one first. I don't care.

Well, violence in terms of hurting people, that's a tactic I wouldn't put in a tool box.

Okay, I see what you're saying: "Violence against people, I don't think that's a tool that I want to put in a tool box." But why?

It is important to understand that as soon as we're strategic, we're not asking only what people want anymore. We aren't talking about a goal for society—now of course we want a non-violent society—but we are talking about what means we are going to utilize to get to a desired society. You understand why I'm saying that? I said, as soon as we're strategic—I mean, if I'm asking you what you're like as a person, then I want to know that you want or don't want violence against people in a new society. And, yes, I want to associate with people who don't want it. But, as soon as I'm asking you about strategy, I'm not asking about your personal wants and dismissals, your tastes, your desires. I'm asking about what you think works and what you think doesn't work.

But think of the drawbacks of violence.

Yes, what are the drawbacks and the assets?

Alienating everybody.

So one drawback would be a negative effect on those you are trying to reach out to. It might be that violence is going to alienate everybody. Does that make sense in the United States?

I think it does. Bombing abortion clinics has alienated people.

It's a fuzzy question. It's a hard question. But one side of the calculation asks about what the issues are when we're trying to figure out strategy. Well, we're always going to include the following: Are we building our support? Are we strengthening our constituency? Are we building organizational structures that lead to what we're trying to accomplish?

Well, there's also the effect on us, which, with violence, is a really important point. What effects does it have on us as organizers and as activists? What does it do to us?

And so on all these counts, we can analyze the thing in question and we can ask whether or not it has negative effects on reaching our constituency, or on building our strength, or on us as people and organizers. But we also might have to look at the setting that we find ourselves in and ask whether we have any choice—whether we have to do it. And if we do, then we know we need to ameliorate the bad aspects because if we don't do that, we lose.

What about Leninist organization? What's the issue there? Well, first of all, what is it? Does anybody know?

It's a vanguard group that does the decision making.

So it's an organizational structure in which you have mind and body, or you have general and troops I suppose is the right analogy in some sense. You have an apparatus that is doing the theory, doing the vision, doing the strategy, figuring out the campaigns, issuing the instructions, hopefully with great emotional appeal. And everybody else does what needs doing. Now, there're some arguments in favor of this. It could be efficient. It could be disciplined. And then there are some arguments against it. It might be that it doesn't lead where you want to go. But can it win?

Yeah. It did.

It did, right. This is not an open question. Some of this stuff we're guessing about and have to be guessing about it, because we have no experience of it. We use what experience we have, the concepts we have, and we come to the best conclusion we can. But in other cases we actually know. The first thing advocates of Leninist organization say is that they have won. So Leninist organizations can win. "Now what's the problem with winning?" they ask their critics. And I say for starters, "Well, win what? The bad guys have won, too.

Winning is not enough to warrant that we employ some approach."
They won the wrong thing.

So winning is not a sole criterion of value. Just like those people
who went into Seattle and declared themselves a liberation front: "We
have created motion and energy. We are wonderful." And they were
wrong. Motion isn't the sole criterion of value. Motion to where?

It isn't the case that every Leninist is a little Hitler or a little
Lenin or a little Stalin. The Leninist might say, "Don't be so paternal
with us. I understand the ills of Leninist organizations. I understand
the ills of hierarchy. I don't like the bad aspects of it any more than
you do. I want the same democratic, participatory end as you want.
But the other side is waving an M-16 at me. And I know this works
and I want to use it not because I enjoy hierarchy and authority, but
because I want to change the world and the other side has created a
setting where nothing that is more in tune with my ultimate values
will succeed. So I have to do this, and I also know I have to guard
against the bad side effects."

All right, that's a sincere discussion. Do you have to use this form?
If you use this form, will it subvert your true desires steadily
substituting new aims for what you thought you were pursuing? And
then we have to discuss the possibility and analyze it and figure out
what the implications of the role structure of these things called
democratic centralism and vanguard party are, and how much they're
likely to become the new state, and all the rest of it. And if you look at
all that and decide not only that Leninism is abstractly morally
inferior to something you'd rather be doing, but also that there is
something else that you can do that is more likely to attain your
desired ends, then you rule Leninism out from your box of tactical
options. That's where I'm at about it—I don't think Leninist organizational options are good options. But I don't feel quite the same way
about violence, though the logic of the discussion is precisely the same,
and my feelings are almost the same. That is, with violence I think
there are times when it is the only option, or it is a worthy and viable

option, as long as we are attuned to the problems and not adopting it as a general persona. With Leninism, I think the choice is almost always a Leninist persona or not, that's the meaning at stake, and I opt against it.

If you're in the United States and trying to make a revolution, one of the things you have to deal with is authoritarianism, I think, due to the character of our four spheres and the mindsets that are associated with reproducing current oppressions as compared to battling against them. So I think you have to address authoritarianism to overcome submission to elite rule, or you're not going to get anyplace. Notice, if you really think that all those four spheres are reproducing each other and you really understand that due to that mutuality you have to deal with all four of them, then you know that you have to deal with the state, and the state's logic and dynamics, and that you have to deal with authoritarianism. But that has strategic implications. You can't counter authoritarianism, eliminate its impact within your projects, and oppose it in society while you are literally reproducing and even celebrating its virtues in your practice and rhetoric.

Do you differentiate between a rejection of Leninism and a rejection of things like leadership and education in relatively small groups and differential commitments?

Of course I do. I'm not against leadership and excellence and working hard and emulating people who set a fine standard. There is nothing wrong with any of that unless those things are done in a way that subverts your values and aims. It's a specific structure that I'm against, a set of institutional roles, a set of allocations of power. And I should say I'm against it in the U.S. not just because I think it would win the wrong thing—authoritarian political forms and coordinator class-dominated economic forms—which is a reason to be against it anywhere. In the U.S. however, I don't think it would win the wrong thing because I doubt it could ever win anything leftist in the U.S. I don't think it could attract sufficient support from the needed constituencies to fight its way out of a paper bag in the U.S. And the reason is because average people are so anti-authoritarian in the U.S., in spirit, but yet so habituated to obedience, in practice, that on both counts it is essential for a left movement to be anti-authoritarian. If you're going leftward in your morals and sense of right and wrong and you're adopting a dissident position allying with those worst off in society, you have to be highly anti-authoritarian in the U.S. And so an approach to organization which emphasizes becoming obedient, and not just to anyone but to exactly the kind of person you are tired of being obedient to, just won't attract wide support and certainly won't counter the dynamics that reproduce the broader oppressions of society. In Third World countries, you can do a Leninist approach and maybe you can garner support and a powerful movement, so you might gain sufficient power to win gains, but the other problem with Leninism then comes into play: that it leads to the wrong end.

So what about violence and the Left?

I think there is more than one side to this question. With violence for me one issue is that in the U.S. if you turn the other cheek, they'll hit that one. And if you sit down on the railroad tracks, they'll run you over. The U.S. is arguably the most violent country in the world in its culture and behavior patterns. And this raises a hard problem for non-violence, obviously. In many settings, violence trumps non-violence. Not always, but sometimes. So it isn't obvious that committing yourself in a principled way to non-violence in all contexts is actually the way to minimize violence. Sometimes the fact that you won't defend yourself literally invites attack. Indeed, in the U.S. I think that an absolute a priori commitment to non-violence most likely guarantees that all the violence will be directed at you and that there may well be enough to squash you. But being willing to defend one's self, in certain situations, is not a prescription for going out and buying M-16s and trying to attack the state, in which case you're squashed in seven seconds. The best way you handle violence is to create a situation in which the social costs of suppressing you with violence are higher than not doing so. (Just as in winning any reform-you see how our conceptual approach just leads to this kind of reasoning, at least to test it and see its viability?)

So that's what you do, I think. And if you don't, you get attacked. You have to set up a situation in which elites lose more than they gain by using their violent apparatus against you. If you can do that, you're dealing with violence well. Sometimes doing this may include being willing to defend yourself, I think. But the point here isn't to decide the issue in some a priori way for all cases. If you're interested in reading people on the side of non-violence as a principled stance you should read Dave Dellinger who is certainly one of the most admirable movement participants in the United States in the past century. He's an unbelievable person and his autobiography is a good thing to read for this and for many topics.

At the other extreme, how many people have heard of Frantz Fanon? He was an African revolutionary who wrote on a lot of topics, of course. He was a psychiatrist, and he had a thesis that violence was therapeutic. Violence for the repressed and the oppressed served the purpose, he said, of liberating their sentiments and freeing them from psychological subservience, and, therefore, it was a positive factor in the movement. For Fanon, or his readers, anyhow, violence wasn't so much a last resort, forced on us by circumstances, as it was actually something to pursue as part of our way of eliminating the vestiges of repressive belief and habit in ourselves. I happen to think this is nonsense and that violence has horrible effects on its perpetrators, more often than not causing them to devalue human life and elevate themselves to a higher status than others—why else do they have the right to exercise this violence? But you see how the issues can be tackled and thought about in diverse and serious ways, rather than folks merely screaming at each other this or that position based on inexpressible intuitions.

Violence and Leninist organizational choices are different things, I think. But in deciding whether we can have them in our menu of available tactics as people trying to improve the world, our reasoning process is similar. For example, we have an understanding of what's wrong now, and of what we want in the future. In our case, let's say, we have an understanding of four spheres of social life with their defining core institutions creating role offerings that circumscribe options and outcomes in horribly oppressive ways. And we understand the emergence of a center of people with beliefs and habits in considerable part created by these impositions, as well as by our fighting against them for immediate changes and long-term changes as well. And let's say we see these four spheres as co-reproducing such that to change any one of them the most sensible orientation is to build movements addressing all four. And we have an understanding of our goals, say, for these four spheres and their interrelations, emphasizing institutional aims that foster and facilitate necessary social functions but also further values we care about—for example, equity, solidarity, diversity, and self management. And we understand something about people and their current conditions, and we see certain constituencies as critical to building movements, and certain patterns of struggle for non-reformist reforms and for infrastructure empowering people and leading toward our goals as a priority.

Okay, so do we use Leninist organization and/or violence within the choices we make? If you think there is something about perpetrating violence that structurally or emotionally or interpersonally contributes to building needed movements, then you probably want to use it. If you think it has some very negative attributes but is required by virtue of the choices of those maintaining oppressive structures, then you may want to use it, but only the minimum possible amount and with careful safeguards against its negative effects. If you think it not only has bad effects but also actually reduces your prospects of being able to ward off the violence of the state or its other means of destroying your efforts, then you will be against the use of violence very nearly unequivocally. A perfectly consistent position, for example, is to think violent attacks against oppressive institutions and agencies are wholly justified and also utterly insane, at least in industrialized societies. That is the way I feel, by and large, so I certainly hope it is consistent.

The same logical calculations apply to evaluating Leninism, or most any other tactical option: national strikes, different types of rhetoric we might use, different choices about focus, different means of structuring our organizations, different ways of dealing with our own failings, different types of demonstration tactic, and so on. And the calculation we make generally results either in our liking something a lot, not liking it but feeling that sometimes we must use it and guard against associated problems, or thinking something is just downright destructive of our intentions.

Here is a little story about violence. Consider one of Che Guevara's tactics. It's an example of thinking about violence in a very ugly context that has nothing whatsoever in common with living in a good society. So Che said, "Look, in any confrontation we're going to have in the jungle fighting against Batista's Cuban army, and we want to make sure of one thing. We want to make sure that the person who was in the front of the enemy's line of march is dead when the battle is over." It was a very simple notion. Whatever else we do, kill that person. Why? So nobody would ever want to be in front. If everybody knows that there's 100% likelihood that the person who's in front is going to be dead, who's going in front? I don't know whether this story is totally accurate, or to what extent it worked or not, although the Cuban army did crumble, and it was confronting a force that was relatively minuscule. The point I want to make, however, is about the kind of thinking this is. It is vile in some sense. And that is a problem, because when you start thinking like this it is very hard to stop. But at the same time I suppose everybody has their heroes, and

Che is one of my heroes. Because I think that in context, the things he did were overwhelmingly warranted, courageous, and impressive.

But to employ a process that leads to people thinking as he did in that case, one could argue the price is too high. We won't be able to create a good society, because if we think as Che did in that case for long enough, we're going to lose our human sensibilities. Or you might say something slightly different which is that all the people that had to think like that, after you win, instead of putting them in positions they can abuse, the first thing that you ought to do with those people is ship them off for a long vacation. I happen to think that's a pretty sensible viewpoint. In other words, if there are things that you have to do, as a movement, about which you could predict in advance the likelihood is that the net result of doing those things is going to be that the perceptions and even values of the people involved are adversely affected by it, well then whatever your goals are, you don't leave the people who did those things any room for subverting desirable outcomes later. (Of course, the irony with Che is that later he seems to have been perhaps the most libertarian voice in the revolution, though not always and not regarding violence.)

How did the Bolsheviks raise money before the war? Does anybody know?

Bank robbery.

Who was the guy who organized the bank robbers? Guess?

Lenin.

No. Lenin was too busy.

Stalin.

Yes, Stalin. So Stalin organized the bank robbers. And that's pretty interesting. There were others involved, of course, but in any case, Stalin did that and I don't think that's an accident. Maybe it was his personality that led to his being involved. Or maybe it was just a dangerous job and he did it out of sincere commitment, despite it being out of character. The thing is, you do stuff like that and your character changes. So am I in principle against robbing banks to get money? No, I'm not against it in principle. If there was a way, tomorrow, that leftists could rip off millions of dollars and have that money available for activist purposes, or even just for redistribution, without the costs being higher than the gains (see, we have to use that accounting system too), I'd be for it. But I wouldn't want to elevate the people doing it to running the movement.

Choosing what to do and how to do it in social contexts, with human stakes, is not simple. It is partly guided by one's view of what exists and what is being sought, partly by one's values and intuitions. It's sometimes hard to pin down.

When I was a student at MIT, others used to ask me if I would burn down a library. This is during the Vietnam War. And the particular situation I was in was that I would often be talking to a large group of students in a big hall, because of the role that I was playing and what I was doing and the particular prominence I had. And among the more sensible and serious queries, students would often ask questions like, "Would you burn down a library to stop the war in Vietnam?" And I would just look at them and say, "Well, you wouldn't? You wouldn't burn down that library right there, right now, to stop the war in Vietnam? Are you telling me that you would not burn 17 books or 17,000 books and some walls and floors in order to stop a war that's killing tens and hundreds of thousands and indeed millions of innocent people? Be serious." And then I would go on to point out that such activity would be worse than mindless, aiding and abetting those pursuing the war, not restraining them.

So in certain contexts there are things that you do that you wouldn't do in a good world, or wouldn't even dream of doing in a good world, but you would do in those contexts. But regarding the people who are doing those things, if it distorts their thinking and values, they need to be treated not as leaders, but as casualties.

Suppose you have spies. So you have some people who are professional liars. What do you do with them after you win? Do you make them the news bureau? Well, that's what happens in history to date. Idiot choices like that. I mean, it doesn't make any sense at all, unless, of course, you intend your news bureau to be an evasive and manipulative institution.

What I am trying to do in this disjointed lecture is to just bring up various examples, issues, and experiences that call forth the kinds of analytic thinking that goes into being strategic and tactical in a sensible way. Not the nonsensical, hyper-inflated, theoretical debates that have no practical meaning, but the kinds of day-to-day concerns that really do arise and really do impact what we do and our success or failure.

Here is another example to contemplate. Again, it is from my past—or distant past, I guess, for many of you—but I think it directly bears on the present, and may allow you to think about the present even more objectively, by being so distant.

In the Sixties, there were people who were just wonderful people who got on a particular trajectory of personal interaction and it wasn't six months before they were sectarian crazies. They're running around at night and they're coming to your house and they're sneaking in the door and saying, "We are the Vietcong." And they really do think they are the Vietcong. I mean, they've simply lost track of reality. Understanding the dynamics by which this kind of devolution of people's awareness happens, by which people can move right past supporting solidarity to indulging in fantasy, isn't some weird diversion from trying to change the world. It is, instead, very much a part of developing a powerful movement.

A movement isn't built solely on understanding how the Bank of America or inflation works, or what patriarchy is, and standing against these ills. That's the easy part. It's also understanding how choices that we make about tactics impact us: how violence, or our ways of organizing ourselves, or our ways of judging ourselves (like criticism/self-criticism), or our forms of arguing, or our modes of reasoning, or our choices of concepts variously impact us and those we are trying to communicate with, as well. But then comes the annoying complication: we can't sensibly go to the opposite extreme of asking everybody to be perfect people overnight, either. We have to have a sense of proportion, of taking insights steadily forward, but not so far forward as to turn them into destructive sectarian norms that are unattainable or way out of reach with reality.

I remember a rather ridiculous sect from my youth, the Progressive Labor Party, that at one time decided that revolution was impeded by many phenomena that distracted people's attention from the struggle. So they developed a new line—no more sex until after they win. You can perhaps imagine how successful that line of exemplary thought was as a recruitment slogan. And perhaps that is a good place to close this chapter, with a note of levity that embodies, however, a very serious point.

Afterword

> Those who profess to favor freedom, and yet deprecate agitation, are men who want crops without plowing up the ground. They want rain without thunder and lightning....Power concedes nothing without a demand. It never did and it never will....Find out just what people will submit to, and you have found the exact amount of injustice and wrong which will be imposed upon them; and these will continue until they are resisted with either words or blows, or with both. The limits of tyrants are prescribed by the endurance of those whom they oppress.
>
> –Frederick Douglass

I hope the preceding chapters have clarified at least somewhat how one can usefully employ, criticize, and even develop a conceptual framework suited to intervention for radical progress. The chapters also presented a specific conceptual framework that I find desirable. What should those who wind up using it, adapting it, and refining it, call it?

In an earlier incarnation, Robin Hahnel and I called the viewpoint complementary holism and even got a group of very sensible and wonderful co-authors—Lydia Sargent, Noam Chomsky, Mel King, Leslie Cagan, and Holly Sklar—to ratify that name in the collectively authored volume, *Liberating Theory*, published by South End Press.

Okay, we were daft in those days. How pretentious the name complementary holism is. But what is a better name? Well, I don't know, but whatever we call it, what we have here, is a Multi-Issue, -Focus, and -Tactic, Growth-Oriented, Revolutionary Perspective. Maybe advocating something called MIFTGORP, which is the best word I could come up with using the various initials, would give us a sense of fallibility, humor, and proportion, to go with our commitment, passion, and focus.

In any event, what is being growth-oriented all about? The other adjectives follow straightforwardly from what we have said so far, but what does growth-oriented mean?

Well, we can have a conceptual framework that is stability-oriented or we can have one that is growth-oriented, and it means we opt for the later. What's the difference?

With the former we would have the intent of showing, over and over, just how clever our perspective is. We would always strive to find that it is wise and insightful—that's the *modus operandi*. We would be disturbed whenever the theory seems unsatisfactory. We would get points, so to speak, and buttress our identity, by showing it is right and by warding off naysayers. We would lose points, and have our identity collapse just a bit, when inadequacies were admitted. Our posture would be to use MIFTGORP aggressively, continually defending it. One way this sort of stability-oriented orientation toward a conceptual framework arises—and I bet from your experience you can attest that it is quite common—is for a framework's concepts and ideas to become equated to our integrity, personality, and worth. Claims of weakness in the conceptual framework sound, to our ears, like claims of weakness in us, and if we are even slightly defensive, we reflexively ward off any doubts about our views as we might ward off doubts about our being. We become stability-oriented.

A growth-oriented conceptual framework, in contrast, is one that urges its own improvement. We seek to find, over and over, how to improve it. We always strive to find its failings and limitations. That's our *modus operandi*. We are disturbed when we can't unearth problems to fix. Our posture is to use our concepts cautiously, and to continually improve them. We don't get points for how often we use it successfully. Instead, we best verify our worth and that of our framework when we find something in it that we can improve. We scour it for inadequacies, always ready to find that some concept needs further work and that some relationship can be understood better than we have heretofore understood it. This quality of having a growth-oriented attitude about one's ideas, rather than a stability-oriented attitude, is the antithesis of sectarianism. Sectarianism is defensive and preservationist and often obscurantist and unconcerned with truth. We need instead to be self-critical and growth-oriented, and to strive for clarity and seek truth as best we can.